Hebron
Journey to our Roots

Hebron: Journey to our Roots
Copyright © 2025 by The Jewish Community of Hebron
All rights reserved.

It is prohibited to use the material in this publication without the express prior permission of the author and the publisher.

For sales inquiries, contact: store@israel365.com

Published by the Jewish Community of Hebron in partnership with Israel365.

Author and Editor: Dr. Noam Arnon
Research Advisor: Aryeh Klein
Content Advisor: Yishai Fleisher
Editorial Board: Uri Karzen, Yishai Fleisher, Tzipi Schlissel, Ori Arnon, Elimelech Karzen, Michael Lixenberg
Language Editor: Emunah Weitzman, Ben Bresky
English Translation: Shelli Karzen
Photos: Gershon Elinson, Hebron archives, David Wilder, Shmuel Mushnick, Dr. Noam Arnon, Yochanan Ben Yaakov, Elisha Grossberg, Chaim Tuitto, Mendy Hartman.

The historical photos of the Jewish Quarter, the Avraham Avinu synagogue, and Beit Hadassah were photographed by Gershon Elinson, who documented the Jewish community of Hebron since its onset.

The slides from the collection of Yochanan Ben Yaakov were scanned by Michael Lixenberg.

The editors have made every effort to locate the source of the images. If an image's source was mistakenly identified, we apologize and will publish the correct source in the next edition.

Cover and interior design by the Virtual Paintbrush.

ISBN 978-1-957109-57-2 (hardcover) • ISBN 978-1-957109-58-9 (paperback)

First Edition 2025

ISRAEL365

www.hebron.org.il   www.Israel365.com

Hebron
Journey to our Roots

A VISITOR'S GUIDE
By Dr. Noam Arnon

ISRA€L365

The printing of this book has been sponsored
by a generous donation from

Meir and Shandee Fuchs

in memory of their parents

Sam and Helen Fuchs

Holocaust survivors who merited
visiting Hebron and contributed
to its rebuilding.

And their grandparents

Rabbi Sholom Klass and Irene Klass

Through their newspaper, *The Jewish Press*,
they contributed and helped to bring awareness
to the rebuilding of Hebron.

Table of Contents

Shalom and Welcome to Hebron! 1

The Cave of Machpelah. 3
 1. Overview 3
    Preface 3
    The Era of the Patriarchs and Matriarchs. 5
    The Early Israelite Era 6
    Second Temple Era: The Monumental Structure . . 7
    The Building on Top of the Cave of Machpelah . . . 8
    End of the Ancient Era and the Middle Ages 11
    Modern Era. 13
 2. A Visit to the Tomb of the Patriarchs and Matriarchs. . 15
    Second Temple Era: The Herodian Structure 16
    The Middle Ages 17
    The Seventh Step 18
 3. A Guided Tour Inside the Tomb of the
    Patriarchs and Matriarchs. 20
    First Entrance. 20
    Arrangement of the Tomb Markers: 21
    The Hall of Abraham and Sarah. 22
    The Hall of Isaac and Rebecca 24
    Division of the Building 26
    Entrance to the Garden of Eden 26

| Exploration of the Cave in the Modern Era 29
| 1968 Exploration............................. 29
| 1981 Exploration 30
| Central Courtyard and Torah Ark................31
| The Hall of Jacob and Leah 33
| The Tomb of Joseph/the Head of Esau 35
| The View of Hebron...........................36

A Visit to Historic Sites in Hebron 40

| Gross Square and King David Street.............41
| The Jewish Quarter and the Avraham Avinu
| Synagogue......................................43
| The 1929 Massacre and the Destruction of the
| Jewish Quarter 46
| The Chabad Synagogue 52
| Beit Romano...................................53
| Hezekiah Quarter – Nachalat Chabad............56
| Beit Hadassah..................................57
| Tel Hebron - The Site of Biblical Hebron.........63
| Admot Yishai Neighborhood 67
| Beit Menachem 69
| The Four-Room House 69
| The Rooftop Observation Point –
| Beit Menachem 70
| The Tomb of Yishai (Jesse) and Ruth..............74
| The Eastern Trail 74
| Abraham's Spring 75

Canaanite Wall / Wall of the Giants..............76
Ancient Olive Trees 78
Ancient Tel Hebron Archeological Site 79

The Western Trail.................................. 83
Chabad Cemetery – Menucha Rachel Section... 89
Grave of Rebbetzin Menucha Rachel Slonim.... 90
Four Sites Specified in the Hebron Accords 90
Elonei Mamre 91
Cave of Otniel Ben Kenaz...................... 92
Eshel Avraham 93
Ein Sarah (Sarah's Spring) 94
Additional Sites............................... 94
Tomb of Abner (Avner) Ben Ner 94
The Alleys of the Old City - The Casbah 95
Interesting Jewish Sites in the Casbah 98

Shalom and Welcome to Hebron!

Hebron is one of the most interesting, central, and important places in Jewish history. It is the site of some of the foundations of human culture. It is known as the City of the Patriarchs and Matriarchs. It is where the Biblical founding fathers and mothers appeared on the world stage, lived, and were buried: Abraham and Sarah, Isaac and Rebecca, Jacob and Leah. These are the roots and foundations of the Jewish nation, the personas who bequeathed humanity its values, and the basis of its culture. Hebron is also the city in which King David, the founder of the kingdom of Judea and one of the greatest and most famous kings in the history of the world, initially established his kingdom.

Hebron is the most ancient city in the Hebron Hills

region. In the Biblical era, it was the capital of Judea, the region where the Jewish nation was forged and fashioned. In the Second Temple period, Hebron's Jewish community preserved unique Jewish traditions. In the Middle Ages, Hebron was home to traditional Jewish communities that cleaved to the City of the Patriarchs and Matriarchs with devotion and lived a life of modesty, camaraderie, and spiritual creativity. In the 20th century, Hebron witnessed revolutionary change. At the beginning of the century, murderous massacres perpetrated by the Arabs of Hebron uprooted the ancient Jewish community from the city. Toward the end of the century, Jews returned to Hebron and renewed the Jewish community in the most ancient Jewish city in the world.

This, in addition to extraordinary archeological discoveries, a fascinating museum, ancient picturesque scenery, and a breathtaking observation point, will provide you with a unique experience.

Enjoy exploring our ancient city!

The Cave of Machpelah

1. Overview

We recommend reading this section in the shade of the olive trees at the entry plaza to the Tomb of the Patriarchs and Matriarchs before entering the building. If time is short, you can skip this overview.

Preface

The Tomb of the Patriarchs and Matriarchs, which houses the Cave of Machpelah, is the most important site in Hebron—and one of the most important sites in the Land of Israel and perhaps in the entire world. It is the burial place of the Patriarchs and Matriarchs of the Jewish nation. They were the founders of faith in one God, a faith accepted by most of humanity.

> *"And after this, Abraham buried Sarah his wife in the cave of the field of Machpelah before Mamre--the same is Hebron--in the land of Canaan. And the field, and the cave that is therein, were made sure unto Abraham for a possession of a burying-place by the children of Heth."*
> – Genesis 23:19-20

The Bible relates that after choosing Hebron as his first home, Abraham bought the Cave of Machpelah as a burial place for his wife, Sarah, and for the heads of the family who would descend from him and perpetuate the nation he was about to found. The Cave of Machpelah became the first Hebrew inheritance in the Land of Israel, the foundation of the Jewish nation and the basis of the Jewish homeland.

A story in the mystical Kabbalistic Jewish tradition relates that the first couple in the world, Adam and Eve, are also buried in the Cave of Machpelah. According to this tradition, Adam felt a mysterious closeness to the Garden of Eden at the site and dug out a cave there so that he could once again be close to the Garden. Hence, the Cave of Machpelah was chosen as the eternal resting place of Adam and Eve. Abraham, who arrived in Hebron approximately 1,000 years later, saw a light emanating from the Cave and smelled the fragrance of the Garden of Eden. For this reason, he chose to make his home in Hebron and acquire the Cave as the final resting place for himself, his wife, and eventually, his family.

The description of the purchase of the Cave of Machpelah

is extensively covered in the Torah (Genesis 23). The description includes the complex negotiations between Abraham and Ephron the Hittite, a respected resident of Canaanite Hebron. Ultimately, Abraham measured four hundred shekels of pure silver into Ephron's hands – a veritable fortune in those days.

The Bible gives a detailed description of the location of the Cave of Machpelah. It is at "the edge of [his] field", "facing Mamre" which is southeast of the historic location of Elonei Mamre (also called Jebel Nimra), in the eastern part of ancient Hebron (today's Tel Hebron). This Biblical description perfectly fits the Cave's modern location as well.

The Era of the Patriarchs and Matriarchs

In the era of the Patriarchs and Matriarchs, which parallels the Middle Bronze Age, about 3,700 to 3,800 years ago, Hebron was a major city fortified by a massive, strong wall. Archeologists have unearthed remnants of the ancient city and additional important discoveries from this era in Tel Hebron (see the description of the Tel in this booklet). The Cave of Machpelah and additional burial caves nearby were situated on the rocky slopes in the eastern part of the city, near the fruitful fields of the Hebron Valley. In the depths of the Tomb of the Patriarchs and Matriarchs building, a burial cave typical of this era was discovered. The word "Machpelah" in Hebrew comes from the word "double." The two sequential caves, connected by an entrance, is likely the "double cave" the Bible describes.

The Hebron Valley. The Cave of Machpelah is prominent in the center.

Genesis includes several descriptions of the Cave of Machpelah. Among them are the stories of the burials of the Patriarchs and Matriarchs: Abraham and Sarah, Isaac and Rebecca, Jacob and Leah. The final chapters of Genesis (49-50) tell of Jacob giving the directive to his sons in Egypt to return him to his homeland and to bury him in the Cave of Machpelah in Hebron. Hence, Jacob, whose name was changed to Israel, became the symbol of the three Patriarchs of the Nation of Israel, who are buried in the Cave of Machpelah.

The Early Israelite Era

The sages relate the tradition that Caleb, one of the heads of the tribe of Judah, recited a prayer at the Cave of Machpelah. In the merit of that prayer, he was saved from the misguided council of his fellow scouts, and later was given Hebron as the capital of his portion in the Land of Israel.

Archeological discoveries show that during the First Temple era (parallel to the Iron Age, about 2,500-3,200 years ago), Hebron was a central city, the capital of the tribe of Judah. The famous member of this tribe, David, was appointed king of Israel while he was still in Hebron and later continued his rule in Jerusalem.

The Tel Hebron archeological site boasts important archeological discoveries from the Early Israelite era (see the description of Tel Hebron later in this booklet). For example, ceramic vessels from the days of the Kingdom of Judea, approximately 2,800-2,900 years ago, were discovered in the depths of the Cave of Machpelah, proving that Jews visited the holy Cave in ancient times, often leaving ceramic vessels in honor of the exalted figures buried there.

Goblets from the First Temple era. A similar goblet was discovered in the depths of the Cave of Machpelah.

Bowls from the First Temple era. A similar bowl was discovered in the depths of the Cave of Machpelah.

Second Temple Era: The Monumental Structure

The monumental structure we know today as the Tomb of the Patriarchs and Matriarchs was built by Herod, the king of Judea under the Roman Empire, during the Second Temple Era (approximately 2,000 years ago). By building the splendid structure above the Cave of Machpelah, Herod, the Jewish king who was descended from an Edomite family that converted to Judaism in the Hasmonean era, emphasized his lineage from the Forefathers and Mothers and his belonging to the Jewish nation. The structure, parallel in style to the walls of the Temple Mount, which was also built during Herod's reign, was built without a roof. This was done to direct the worshiper's gaze to Heaven and prevent an errant prayer to any other entity.

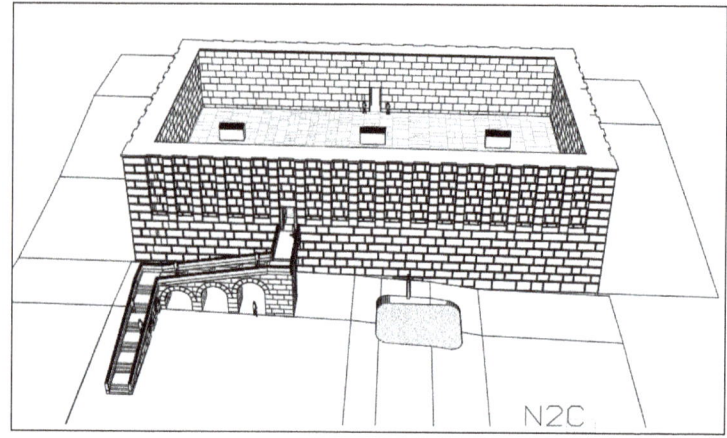

Sketch of the Tomb of Machpelah
Credit: Yerachmiel Weiss, architect

The Building on Top of the Cave of Machpelah

To make it possible to erect the structure on top of the Cave, an impressive retaining wall about 10 meters high was constructed at the base of the hill to the south, and a low retaining wall was built to the north. Walls measured to the hill's incline were built to the east and west. Domes were constructed between the walls, and a massive floor was laid upon them. The entire area, approximately 60x35 meters, was surrounded by additional walls about ten meters high.

The Tomb of Machpelah design is similar to the Biblical Tabernacle, and combines elements of classic Hellenist-Roman style mausoleums.

In its design, the structure combines the Jewish style of the Tabernacle, surrounded by pillars and curtains, with the classic Hellenist-Roman style of the mausoleum, an elegant burial chamber for important people.

Six memorial monuments were built inside the building in memory of the three Biblical Patriarch and Matriarch couples. Rachel, Jacob's other wife, was buried in Bethlehem. The monuments were placed symmetrically: Abraham and Sarah in the middle, Isaac and Rebecca to their right, and Jacob and Leah to their left. Apparently, the entrances to the building were on the top floor, which were accessed by stairs and constructed on top of arches and domes, similar to the Temple Mount.

In the Second Temple era, the spiritual life of the Jewish nation revolved primarily around the Temple. After the destruction of the Temple (70 CE), however, and particularly following the Bar Kochba rebellion (132-135 BCE), Jews were not allowed to enter Jerusalem and its surroundings. During that era, Jews searched for additional ways to live according to their religion and spirit and continue to bask in the feeling of Divine Presence.

In addition to studying the Bible and praying, Jews sought a deeper connection with God by visiting the burial site of the Patriarchs and Matriarchs, the harbingers of faith in the one God. This site became a sacred place, offering encouragement and inspiration. The structure, a symbol of Jewish national memory, served as a holy place for visits, prayer, and spiritual inspiration, imbued with the enduring faith of the Forefathers and Foremothers.

Rabbinical sources, including the Mishnah, Midrash, Zohar, and Talmud, are replete with statements highlighting the centrality and importance of the Patriarchs and Matriarchs and the Cave of Machpelah. One significant statement is, "The Patriarchs are the chariot of the Shechinah (God's Divine Presence)."[1] This and other similar statements testify to the religious and spiritual importance of the Cave of Machpelah in Jewish tradition.

The Talmud discusses the meaning of the term "Machpelah," which means double. This shows that the sages were familiar with the building and the tunnels beneath it.[2] In the writings of the sages there are allusions to prayer in the Cave of Machpelah,[3] of a visit deep inside of the Cave[4] and of the arrangement of the tomb markers inside the building that parallel their current placement.

True to these sources, the names of Jewish worshipers who visited the Cave during the period of the sages (4th and 5th century BCE), mostly written in Greek and some in Hebrew, were discovered etched into the walls of the Cave of Machpelah.

---

1 Bereishit Rabah 83 et al.

2 Babylonian Talmud, Eruvin 53a

3 Babylonian Talmud, Sotah 34b

4 Babylonian Talmud, Baba Batra 58a

End of the Ancient Era and the Middle Ages

During the Byzantine era (4th - 7th century, between 1,300 and 1,700 years ago) Christianity was the official religion of the Roman Empire. The Land of Israel also became important in Christian theology. Christian interest in Hebron was initially focused on the site known as Mamre in the city's northern section. About 1,500 years ago, a church was built inside the Cave of Machpelah. Sources and sojourners testify that Jews and Christians would pray side-by-side inside the building: the Christians (according to Christian custom) would face east, while the Jews would face north (in the direction of Jerusalem).

A synagogue continued to exist inside the building atop the Cave of Machpelah into the Muslim Era (7th–10th centuries, 900 to 1,300 years ago) and even during the Ayyubid and Crusader eras (11th–12th century, 800 to 900 years ago).

During the Middle Ages, Jews continued to visit the Cave of Machpelah and pray there. One of the most famous visitors was Maimonides, Rabbi Moses ben Maimon, who visited and prayed in the Cave of Machpelah in 1165. In a letter, he described his experience as follows:

> *"On the third day of the week, the fourth day of the month of MarCheshvan, in the year six and twenty to Creation, we left Acco to make the dangerous journey to Jerusalem, and I entered the great and Holy House, and I prayed in it on Thursday, the sixth day of the month of MarCheshvan. And on the first day of the week, the ninth of the month, I left Jerusalem for Hebron to kiss the graves of my Forefathers*

in the Cave. And on that day I stood in the Cave and I prayed, praise God for all.
                                    MAIMONIDES

Another visitor was Benjamin of Tudela, the famous Jewish traveler who visited the Land of Israel during his travels between 1160 and 1173.

In 1265, the Mamluks conquered the Land of Israel. They added towers to the monument's walls and turned the holy site into a Muslim mosque. In addition, a structure was added next to the southern wall, which the Muslims called "the Tomb of Joseph." According to the Bible and Jewish tradition, the actual Tomb of Joseph is in Shechem.

Jewish notables at the Seventh Step, 1907. The sign on the gate bans them from entering.

In 1267, the Mamluk Sultan Baibars decreed that Jews and Christians were no longer allowed to enter the building over the Cave of Machpelah. This prohibition remained in place for 700 years. Rather than entering the building and praying inside, Jews were only allowed to stand next to the seventh step of the stairs on the eastern side of the building. A few Jews did manage to enter the building, at great danger to their lives, either in disguise or after paying a hefty sum.

Modern Era

For 700 years, rulers and regimes came and went in the Land of Israel. The Jewish community in Hebron experienced fateful events. Turkish rule replaced Mamluk rule in 1517, and later, Turkish rule was replaced with British rule in 1917.

In 1929, a Jihadist Arab mob attacked the Jews in a pogrom that is known as the Hebron Massacre. The mob murdered 67 Jews and wounded numerous more, two of whom later died of their injuries. The survivors were expelled from Hebron. In 1948, Hebron, like the Old City of Jerusalem and the areas of Judea and Samaria, was conquered by Jordan. During this period, the prohibition against Jews and Christians entering the site remained in place. The Jews, downtrodden but faithful, continued to pray at the Seventh Step.

The Defense Minister and IDF officers at the gate of the Cave of Machpelah following its liberation
Credit: Moshe Milner, Government Press Office
June 8, 1967

In 1967, a very significant historic event unfolded in the Land of Israel. Egypt, Jordan, and Syria declared war on the State of Israel, with the explicit goal of destroying it. Fighting for its existence, Israel merited a glorious victory and liberated parts of its historic homeland, including Judea

Rabbi Shlomo Goren raising the Israeli flag over the gate of the Cave of Machpelah

and Samaria. On June 7, 1967 (28 Iyar, 5727) the historic declaration "the Temple Mount is in our hands" was heard around the world. The Jewish nation returned to its holy city and historic capital in Jerusalem. On that same day, the Jordanian Legion retreated from Hebron, in the Judea region. The next day, Hebron was liberated by the Jerusalem Brigade. The Chief Rabbi of the Israel Defense Forces, Rabbi Shlomo Goren, hung the Israeli flag at the gate of the Tomb of the Patriarchs & Matriarchs. The words of Jeremiah, "and the children shall return to their borders" (Jeremiah 31:16) were fulfilled.

Following the liberation of Hebron, the Tomb of the Patriarchs and Matriarchs was opened for people of all faiths. For decades, various arrangements were made to accommodate these visits and prayers, and the building was divided between Jews and Muslims. Despite various difficulties with transportation and accessibility, the Tomb of the Patriarchs and Matriarchs has become one of the most visited sites in Israel, and the numbers are constantly increasing. In 2019, one million people visited the site. (This number includes visitors of all faiths.)

Tourists at the Tomb of the Patriarchs and Matriarchs

2. A Visit to the Tomb of the Patriarchs and Matriarchs

The visit begins at the entrance plaza, next to the olive trees. An information booth and restrooms are at the foot of the stairs.

The outdoor plaza has benches and shade. It is a good place to rest and read the explanations in this booklet. It is also a good place to look at the building and the findings from various eras.

A large water cistern from the Second Temple Era in front of the Tomb of the Patriarchs and Matriarchs

Second Temple Era: The Herodian Structure

The impressive structure represents the advanced construction capabilities of the Jewish nation during the reign of Herod, King of Judea, who excelled at high-quality, extraordinary stone construction.

Approximately 2,000 years ago, King Herod built many monumental structures both within and outside the Land of Israel. Among them are the expanded Temple Mount, his grand renovation of the Second Temple, and the large, state-of-the-art port in Caesarea. The only structure that has remained whole and active from that era is the edifice above the Cave of Machpelah, standing before us.

The first description of the structure appears in the writings of the Jewish historian Yosef Ben Matityahu (Josephus Flavius), of the 1st century CE. He particularly notes the tomb markers and the superb stone construction. The building is constructed in the magnificent Herodian style. The construction quality is excellent, and the weight of the rocks reach tens of tons. The lower foundation level is reminiscent of the wall of the Temple Mount, particularly the Western Wall. This level includes the cave itself and is sealed and closed. Visitors cannot enter this level. Instead, they ascend to the level above it, where the tomb markers of the Patriarchs and Matriarchs stand and where worshipers gather for prayer and religious ceremonies. Jewish tradition attaches great importance and significance to prayer at the Cave of Machpelah. The memory and merit of the Forefathers are a central theme in Jewish prayer throughout history.

After 2,000 years, the Tomb of the Patriarchs and Matriarchs still stands in a complete state and continues to be active. It is a rare and pronounced example of the architectural magnificence of ancient Jewish construction.

Prayers, weddings, and festivals at the Tomb of the Patriarchs and Matriarchs

The Middle Ages

Construction in the Tomb of the Patriarchs and Matriarchs during the Middle Ages reflects the inclination to include Abraham in the various religious traditions that ruled in the Land of Israel. This era saw additions added to the original Jewish structure.

Above the eastern wall is a section of a church that was added during the Crusader era (12th century). Today, it serves as the main room of the mosque and one can see its gray roof above the original Herodian structure.

In the 13th century, Muslim Mamluks added minarets to the building and a structure on the southern wall called the

Yusefiya, which Muslims consider the Tomb of Joseph. However, the Biblical account, and Jewish tradition, places the Tomb of Joseph in Shechem (Nablus).

The Tomb of the Patriarchs and Matriarchs, with later additions built adjacent to and above it. (Photo from the Jordanian era)

In 2021, archeological excavations began in the Tomb of the Patriarchs and Matriarchs plaza to allow for the paving of an accessibility path. These excavations uncovered houses and water reservoirs from the Middle Ages and the Crusader and Mamluk periods.

Excavations that took place from 2021 to 2022 revealed a residential neighborhood from the Middle Ages. Note the pool in the center of the photo.

The Seventh Step

In the right corner of the structure, there is a small prayer area above several steps and a wooden deck. Today, this area is called the Seventh Step garden, named for the location of the seventh step in a flight of stairs once used to enter the building.

Following the Mamluk conquest in 1267, the Muslim

occupiers imposed a decree that prohibited Jews and Christians from entering the building. The Jews were allowed to stand outside, next to the seventh step at the entrance to the building. There was a gate at that spot and stairs ascending to the entrance at the upper level. The Muslims would go up those stairs to the entrance to the building, while it was prohibited for the Jews to ascend beyond the seventh step. Despite ongoing discrimination and humiliation at the hands of the Muslims, the Jews persevered with wondrous loyalty for 700 years. It was only after the liberation of Hebron during the 1967 Six-Day War that Jews and all other non-Muslims were able to enter the Tomb of the Patriarchs and Matriarchs once again.

Left: Entrance to the Tomb complex. Right: Jews were restricted to ascending only to the seventh step. Credit: The Life of the Jews in Palestine, 1913

In 1968, after a terrorist threw a grenade at Jewish visitors at the Seventh Step, IDF Chief of Central Command, General Rechavam Ze'evi, gave orders to destroy the gate and steps. General Ze'evi recalled how, when he was a child, the Arab guard slapped him for going past the Seventh Step. This area, where Jews prayed for 700 years, has become a symbol of Jewish perseverance and dedication to Hebron and the Cave of the Patriarchs and Matriarchs. Many people continue to pray there.

After reading the introduction about the Tomb's exterior and surroundings, let us go up the stairs or use the elevator and enter the building itself.

3. A Guided Tour Inside the Tomb of the Patriarchs and Matriarchs

First Entrance

To enter the building, we will ascend the steps or use the elevator, which was added in 2023. Upon entering the building, we see a room to the right which contains a Torah ark and is used for Jewish services, brit milah celebrations and other Jewish holiday gatherings. This part of the building is an addition built in the 13th century. The entrance to the original Herodian structure, built 2,000 years ago is in front of us. The addition was called the Yusefiya as per a later Arabic tradition, according to which Joseph, the son of Jacob, was also buried in the Cave of Machpelah.

According to the Bible, the Tomb of Joseph is in Shechem. It has been identified for thousands of years in the Jewish and Samaritan traditions.

The opening in the original wall before us is not the original gate to the structure. It is an opening created during the Crusader era, in the 12th century, to connect the building with a Crusader fortress built to the south.

This wall gives us an insight into ancient construction methods. Two parallel walls of hewn stones were constructed, with mortar and stones filled in between them. This method afforded the structure strength and flexibility in the face of earthquakes and changes in weather. The total breadth of the wall is over two and a half meters (over 8 feet). We will pass the wall and turn right.

To our right, we see an entrance to a room with a tomb marker, attributed to Joseph in the Muslim tradition. This site will be described in greater detail as we exit.

Above us, on the left, we see decorative windows from the Ottoman era and many six-pointed stars, which later became a ubiquitous Jewish symbol, the Star of David.

Let us continue straight and then turn left. We will pass through a gate. On our right we will see the tomb marker of Abraham.

Arrangement of the Tomb Markers:

Leah	Sarah	Rebecca
Jacob	Abraham	Isaac

The order of the tomb markers
Image: Shmaya Mushnick

The Hall of Abraham and Sarah

On the right is a large opening. Inside are the tomb markers of the patriarch Abraham and matriarch Sarah. Here we also see an ark that contains Torah scrolls and other ritual items. In the original Herodian structure atop the Cave of Machpelah, six tomb markers were built on the upper level to symbolize and denote the Patriarchs and Matriarchs interred in the depths of the underground cave. The tomb markers were built symmetrically. The central couple bear the names Abraham and Sarah, the eastern couple, Isaac and Rebecca, and the western couple, Jacob and Leah. However, no tomb markers were constructed for Adam and Eve, whose burial in the Cave of Machpelah is not mentioned explicitly in the Bible but appears in Jewish sources such as the Midrash, Talmud, Zohar, and various travel diaries. The placement of the tomb markers opposite one another symbolizes the founding couples and reflects the importance and sanctity of the marriage bond and family in Jewish tradition.

Abraham and Sarah are particularly important to followers of the Abrahamic faiths. Sarah was the first person to be interred in the Cave of Machpelah, and the entire site was purchased and established in her merit and in her memory. The tomb marker of Abraham, which is in the center of the compound, is built directly on top of the original burial cave complex which is underneath the building.

Prayer at Abraham's tomb marker

The memory and merit of the Forefathers is a central motif in the Bible and Jewish prayer. For example, the Bible relates that Moses said in his prayer, "remember Abraham, Isaac and Israel, Your servants to whom You vowed and said to them 'I will multiply your offspring like the stars of the heavens and all this Land that I said I will give to your offspring - and they will inherit it for eternity" (Exodus 32:13). The Silent Prayer (Amida), the most central and important in the prayer book, recited three times a day, opens with the words: "Blessed are You, Lord, our God, the God of our Forefathers, the God of Abraham, the God of Isaac and the God of Jacob."

The original markers and the walls of the room are decorated with Islamic inscriptions that were added during the Mamluk era to lend Islamic character to the site. The inscriptions include verses from the Koran and inscriptions that memorialize various Mamluk rulers. The State of Israel has left these inscriptions intact and has not changed the hall's Islamic décor. Entrance into the chambers that house the tomb markers is prohibited to Jews and is allowed only for the members of the Islamic *Waqf*.

Abraham's tomb marker

The Hall of Isaac and Rebecca

Let us exit the Abraham and Sarah Hall and turn right until the end of the corridor.

The Hall of Isaac and Rebecca

We are standing at a metal door that separates us from the Hall of Isaac and Rebecca. Usually, the hall is reserved for Muslims and closed to Jews. This large, ornate and impressive hall was enhanced in the Crusader era as a church basilica in the southern part of the original Herodian structure. Later, in the Mamluk era (13th century), the hall was turned into a mosque. It houses the tomb markers of Isaac and Rebecca, around which small memorial structures were built in the Mamluk era. This hall also houses the narrow opening leading to the underground passageway connected to the actual cave complex and burial chambers below the building.

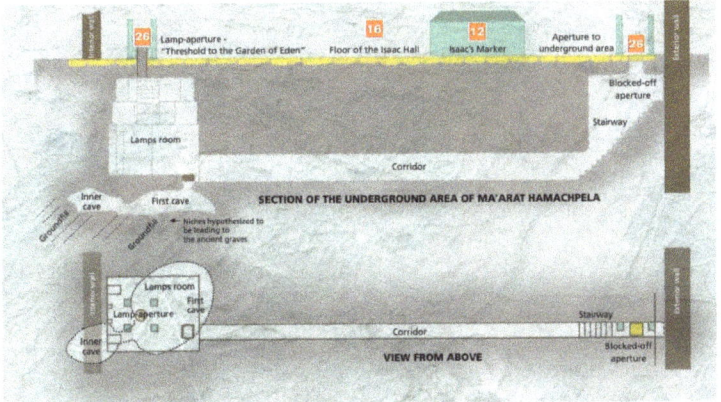

The underground system - cross-section

Prayer in the Hall of Isaac and Rebecca

Division of the Building

Today, the Tomb of the Patriarchs and Matriarchs building, measuring about 2,000 square meters, is divided into separate Jewish and Muslim sections with separate entrances. The area reserved for Muslims includes the Hall of Isaac and Rebecca and the Jau'liyah Hall. The small tomb marker chambers are open only to the Islamic *Waqf*.

As part of a rotation agreement, there are ten non-consecutive days a year when the entire site is reserved for Muslim worshipers, corresponding to Islamic holidays, and ten non-consecutive days a year when the site is reserved for Jewish worshipers. On these days, the Hall of Isaac and Rebecca is open, and tens of thousands of Jews come to pray at the site and view the entrance to the burial cave below the building. One of these special days is known as Shabbat Chayei Sarah, when Jews read the Torah portion that recounts Sarah's passing and Abraham's purchase of the cave and land which would become the Tomb of the Patriarchs and Matriarchs (Genesis 23).

Shabbat Chayei Sarah 2022. Credit: Chaim Tuitto

Entrance to the Garden of Eden

On the western side of the Hall of Isaac and Rebecca is a canopy covering a round opening on the floor. This opening leads to a shaft leading to an underground cave, the actual Cave of Machpelah. The cave was concealed for many generations, arousing curiosity and lending the site a sense of mystery. Even today, after its discovery, the research on the site is fascinating and challenging.

The candle opening that leads to the underground tunnels

There are two canopies in the Hall of Isaac and Rebecca that mark the two entrance passages to the inner cave below.

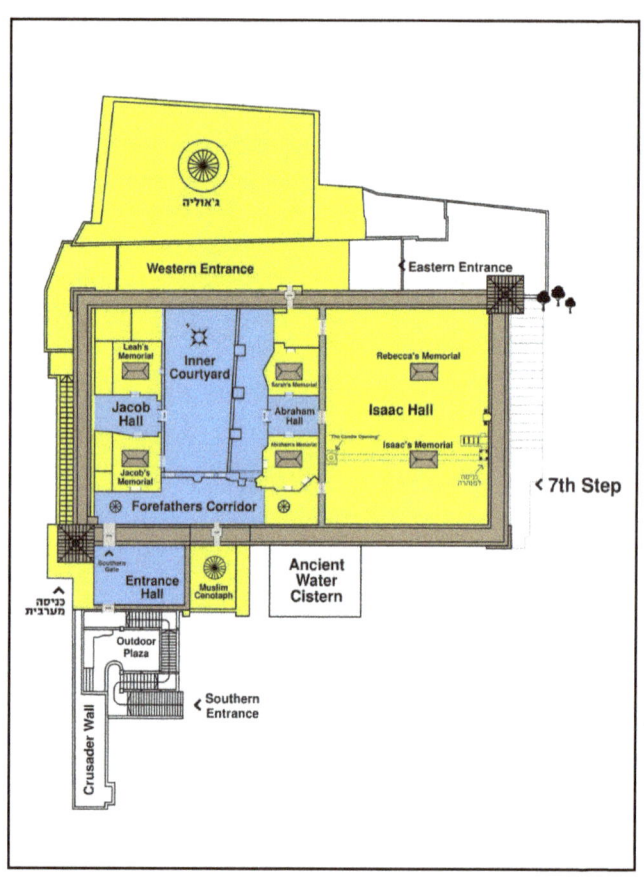

Diagram of the layout of the Tomb of the Patriarchs and Matriarchs

Legends dating back to the Middle Ages claim that those who dared enter the underground cave would not come out alive. One such story is told about the great Kabbalist of Hebron, Rabbi Avraham Azulai (1570 - 1643), author of the renowned book Chesed L'Avraham. At that time, a visiting Ottoman sultan came to see the Tomb of the Patriarchs and Matriarchs. When he bent over to peer into the opening of the cave, his sword, studded with precious stones, slipped and fell deep inside.

The sultan ordered one of his soldiers tied to a rope and lowered him inside to retrieve the sword. However the soldier did not come out alive. Neither did a second soldier who suffered a similar fate. Finally, the frustrated sultan demanded that a Jew be sent down to retrieve the sword, lest the Jewish community be destroyed. The elderly and venerated Rabbi Azulai volunteered for the job. When he was lowered into the cave, he was shocked to be greeted by an elderly man who identified himself as the Biblical Eliezer, servant of Abraham. Eliezer then escorted Rabbi Azulai to another room where he saw the Patriarchs. The rabbi asked if he could stay with them, but they replied that the sword needed to be returned and promised he would join them soon. Rabbi Azulai returned the sultan's sword given to him by the Patriarchs and the Jewish community was spared. He spent the day celebrating and teaching his students Torah and Kabbalah. The next day his soul was returned to his Maker and the rabbi was reunited with the Patriarchs in the next world.

Exploration of the Cave in the Modern Era

1968 Exploration

In 1968 (5728), Defense Minister Moshe Dayan asked his friend and colleague Yehuda Arbel to help explore the entrance to the cave. Arbel chose his twelve-year-old daughter Michal, with whom he had explored caves before, as the only person who could fit down into the narrow opening. Michal discovered an underground room from which a long tunnel extended. She walked the entire length of the tunnel and then saw stairs. Michal ascended the stairs and reached a rock that blocked the entrance from the other side of the hall. She returned through the tunnel, was pulled out of the shaft by a rope, and emerged safe and sound.

1981 Exploration

In 1981 (5741), a group of guides and researchers from Midreshet Hebron (including the author of this booklet, Dr. Noam Arnon) successfully entered the tunnel from the other side of the hall and discovered the inner cave. The exploration took place at midnight during *Slichot* prayers. They descended into the underground tunnel system and then descended to a lower level, where they discovered a double cave, the entrance to which was carved from the rock. Crawling in the cave, they found themselves in the midst of human bones. Overcoming their trepidation, they continued into the depths of the cave, where they discovered pottery which was later identified as being from the era of the Judean Kingdom (dated 8th - 9th century BCE, the First Temple era). After this initial exploration, another delegation, which included IDF officers and an archeologist, entered the next day. They measured and documented the cave, the shape of which was found to be similar to burial caves from the Bronze Age, the era of the Forefathers and Mothers (18th century BCE). Researchers believe the pottery was placed there in previous generations in honor of the Ancestors.

Pottery found in the cave.   *A chalice similar to the one discovered in the cave.*

*Vessels discovered in the cave.
Bottom right: The inner cave*

These discoveries lent additional validity to the identification of the cave as the Biblical Cave of Machpelah and the multi-layered traditions that developed over the millennia.

Due to protests from the Islamic *Waqf*, the cave complex below the Herodian structure has been closed and no visitation or research has been allowed.

Central Courtyard and Torah Ark

We return to the central courtyard of the building which serves as the main Jewish prayer area. A cloth canopy covers most of this space today. Originally, the entire building had no roof and worshipers would turn their eyes upward and direct their prayers to God. Today most of the building is covered. Only the front section of the courtyard remains open.

At the front of the courtyard synagogue, there is a large

and unique Torah ark. It is built out of three different types  of material that symbolize the three Forefathers. The wood symbolizes Abraham, who settled in the forest known as Elonei Mamre near Hebron and hosted guests under the oak tree there. The bronze represents the knife of the Binding of Isaac, and the stone symbolizes Jacob, who placed a stone under his head when he had his dream of the ladder and who is called "the rock of Israel" in the Bible. On the doors of the Torah ark there is a tablet on which is written: "Is the entire eastern sky illuminated even to Hebron?" The source of this inscription is in the Mishnah, in tractate *Tamid* and tractate *Yoma*, which describe the service in the Holy Temple in Jerusalem:

> **The appointed** *priest* **said to** *the other priests:* **Go out and observe if** *it is day and* **the time for offering** *has* **arrived. If** *the time has* **arrived, the observer says: There is light [*barkai*]! Matitya ben Shmuel says** *that the appointed priest phrased his question differently:* **Is the entire eastern sky illuminated even to Hebron? And** *the observer* **says: Yes.**

The service in the Temple began each day with these words, and according to Talmudic sources, this mention of Hebron was meant to arouse the merit of the Forefathers.

Inside the ark are Torah scrolls with covers fashioned according to the customs of both Asheknazic and Sephardic traditions. This is an unusual phenomenon, for generally

 every synagogue prays according to the custom of one particular tradition. The different types of Torah scrolls in the Tomb of the Patriarchs and Matriarchs symbolizes the connection between all the traditions and opinions in the Jewish nation. The Jewish ancestors connect and unite all their sons and daughters to their common roots.

The Hall of Jacob and Leah

From the courtyard, we will enter the Hall of Jacob and Leah, which is between the tomb markers of Jacob and Leah and is another place for prayer in the Tomb of the Patriarchs and Matriarchs. Entry to the tomb marker chambers is closed to Jews. Jacob and Leah have a special connection to Hebron, the capital of Judea. Leah was the mother of Judah, the tribe that settled in greater Hebron in the Biblical era and made Hebron its capital. Jacob passed away in Egypt, but before his death, he directed his son Joseph and then his other sons to bury him in the Cave of Machpelah with his father and grandfather. These are essentially the last words of the last Forefather, Jacob:

> *And he charged them, and said to them: 'I am to be gathered unto my people; bury me*

with my fathers in the cave that is in the field of Ephron the Hittite.

In the cave that is in the field of Machpelah, which is before Mamre, in the land of Canaan, which Abraham bought with the field from Ephron the Hittite for a possession of a burial place.

There they buried Abraham and Sarah his wife; there they buried Isaac and Rebecca his wife; and there I buried Leah.

The field and the cave that is therein, which was purchased from the children of Heth.'

And when Jacob made an end of charging his sons, he gathered up his feet into the bed, and expired, and was gathered unto his people.

(Genesis 49:29-33)

In his final words to his twelve sons, Jacob emphasized the connection between the Jewish people and the Forefathers and Mothers interred in Hebron throughout the generations.

The Bible relates that Jacob was also the first person to be called Israel (Genesis 35:10). The transition from the name Jacob to the name Israel symbolizes the transition of the Jewish nation from a lowly place near the heel (the Hebrew name for Jacob, Yaakov shares a root with the Hebrew word for 'heel' – *akev*) to a lofty, worthy place, a place of triumph and new consciousness. "For you have striven with God and man, and you have prevailed" (Genesis

32:29). The name "Israel" is the name given to the Nation of Israel, the Land of Israel, the Torah of Israel, and in our generation, the State of Israel and all its institutions: the government of Israel, the Knesset of Israel and more. The raising of the flag of Israel over the Tomb of the Patriarchs and Matriarchs during the liberation of Hebron in 1967 symbolized the children returning to their parents, heralding their reunion and restoring the name Israel to its original place of honor.

The name "Israel" inscribed on an ossuary shard from the Hebron area. This is currently the only known appearance of this name found in artifacts discovered from the Second Temple era. (Land of Judea Museum, Kiryat Arba)

The Tomb of Joseph/the Head of Esau

We exit the building from where we came in, and once again pass by the tomb marker from the Middle Ages, called by Muslims Joseph's Tomb, in the Yusefiya Hall. As we know from the Bible, the Biblical Joseph was interred in Shechem (Joshua 24:32). His burial site has been preserved throughout the generations in the Jewish and Samaritan traditions. Some Midrashic sources tie this tomb marker to Esau, whose head was buried in the Cave of Machpelah when he attempted to prevent the burial of Jacob there (*Talmud Bavli Sotah 13a*).

This opening in the wall is one of the two original gates into the building. Visitors would access these gates by means of a large external staircase which was attached to the building. The gate was closed in the Mamluk era and the Yusefiya building, which was covered entirely with marble and Islamic decorations, was built adjacent to it.

The View of Hebron

As we exit the building, we will see the elevator built in 2023. From here, we can view the eastern part of the Hebron Valley. This valley is mentioned in the Bible and used to be covered with fields, vineyards, and orchards. Today, part of it is covered with buildings dating from the Middle Ages, while part of its original agricultural status has been preserved. Opposite us, we see the southern ridge of the Hebron Hills, which serves as the city's southern border. To our right, we see a wall that is the remnant of a fortress built in the Crusader era, adjacent to the Tomb of the Patriarchs and Matriarchs. We will descend the stairs and pass the hospitality area, where visitors are often treated to refreshments. After we pass through the plaza and reach the street below, we can see at the foot of the steps an information center with pamphlets about Hebron and local sites. To our right is the Gutnick Center which features a restaurant and gift shop. Across the street, there is a grassy area. At the far end of it are stairs that lead down to a parking lot. If we turn right and walk for a few minutes, we will reach additional sites of interest, including the historic Jewish Quarter, the Avraham Avinu synagogue, the Hebron Museum in Beit Hadassah, ancient Tel Hebron and more.

Accessibility elevator built in 2023

Information Center

Gutnick Center gift shop and restaurant

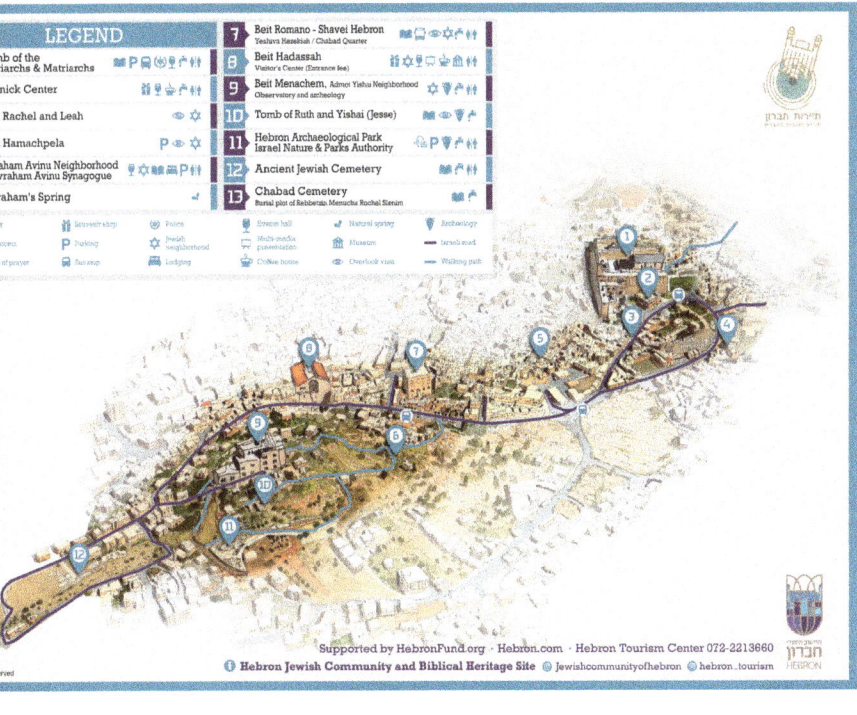

A Visit to Historic Sites in Hebron

WE WILL TURN right and walk along Emek Hebron Street. This street was the southern border of Hebron during the Middle Ages. Since the city was no longer surrounded by a wall, a continuum of buildings were built to provide defense against marauders. Most of the openings between the buildings were added in a later era. On our right, we will see two buildings called Beit Rachel and Beit Leah. The Harchivi Makom Aholech organization purchased these buildings, and today, Jewish families live there, with Arab families living next door.

*A Hebron street, 1922
Credit: Central Zionist Archives*

To our left, we can see a group of buildings surrounding Sarah's Pool (sometimes called King David's Pool and later the Sultan's Pool). This was the main water pool in Hebron during the Middle Ages, originally built during the Muslim conquest and restored during the Crusader era. The pool gathered water that flowed through the Hebron Valley, but since the 1970s, the flow has been stopped, and all that remains is a large winter puddle.

A 19th century picture of the pool (sometimes called King David's Pool.)

Gross Square and King David Street

Gross Square is named in memory of Aharon Gross, a student from the Shavei Hevron yeshiva who was murdered by a terrorist at that spot in 1983 (5743). In the center of the square, there is a monument in his memory. Across the street is an empty structure once used as market stalls. This structure was built on the property of the Jewish Quarter that stood here from the Middle Ages until the Hebron massacre of 1929. After the Jordanian occupation in 1948 (5708), the local Arab leadership and the Jordanian government attempted to erase the remnants of the Jewish

Quarter. To this end, they destroyed the synagogue and other Jewish-owned buildings, and built a marketplace on the property that the Jewish community had purchased over 200 years earlier. After Israel regained the area, they built a new, modern marketplace in the western part of the city, but due to pressure from Arab nationalists, the Arab merchants refused to move there. The frequent terrorist gunfire that was aimed at this area during the Second Intifada chased most of the Arab merchants away, and the market was closed.

Initially, the Jewish community attempted to return to their property and lived in the abandoned market stalls, but they were eventually evicted as a result of pressure from the US government. Since then, the buildings have stood empty, waiting for the construction of a new neighborhood that will rejuvenate the ancient Jewish Quarter.

From here, we can enter the ancient Jewish Quarter and see the Avraham Avinu synagogue, or continue down King David Street to the Hebron Museum in Beit Hadassah. The stores on this street were closed as a security measure following a rash of terrorist attacks here in the early 2000s.

Prior to the division of the city in the Hebron Accords in 1997, this street was bustling with activity. The stores that used to be here were closed and moved to Hebron's new, modern shopping area about a kilometer west, in an area under the control of the Palestinian Authority. Entry into this part of the city is prohibited to Jews, but allowed for non-Jewish tourists. Jews can view the area from a lookout point at the peak of Tel Hebron.

In 2021, Israel's government authorized the beginning of the rebuilding of the southern section of the Jewish Quarter, slated to house a Jewish neighborhood and a tourist area.

PA controlled Hebron – A wealthy, prosperous city experiencing a surge of construction – as viewed from the lookout in Tel Hebron

The Jewish Quarter and the Avraham Avinu Synagogue

We are entering the old Jewish Quarter of Hebron, which has stood at this site since the Middle Ages (approximately 800 years ago). At the center of the quarter was a communal courtyard. The Avraham Avinu Synagogue stands at the side of the courtyard. It was constructed in 1540 by Jewish immigrants who had been expelled from Spain and resettled in the Land of Israel, specifically in Hebron.

The synagogue structure is supported by pillars, with seating for worshippers arranged around the center. Two Torah arks stand along the northern wall, though today only the main ark is in use. At the center of the synagogue is an elevated platform, above which is a dome with windows illuminating the interior. This floor plan was common in ancient synagogues in the Middle East, particularly in the Land of Israel. There are structures with similar floor plans in Jerusalem, Tzfat, and Tiberias.

"Avraham Avinu Synagogue Hebron" by famous Israeli artist Nahum Gutman

Local tradition attributes the name of the synagogue to a legend about the Biblical Abraham, who miraculously appeared to serve as the tenth man for the prayer quorum for the Yom Kippur services.

About 400 years ago, the Jewish community in Hebron was small. A number of community members had to journey far from their homes to earn their livelihood. On Yom Kippur eve, the community gathered in the synagogue for prayers and saw that they had only nine men. They were missing one man to form a prayer quorum (*minyan*). They went out to the street to try to find a tenth man but to no avail. As the sun began to set, they began the preparatory prayers with heavy hearts, knowing that the full services could not be completed without the required number of participants. Suddenly, a Jewish man with a glowing face appeared at the entrance to the synagogue. They asked him if he would like to have something to eat before the fast, but he declined. With joy in their hearts, they began the Yom Kippur prayers. The guest remained standing the entire time, absorbed in his prayers, with an aura of sanctity surrounding him. When the holy day was over, everyone wished to invite this unique guest to break the fast at their home. They cast lots to determine who would merit this honor, and the lot fell upon the synagogue caretaker. But as they were walking through the city's narrow alleyways, the honored guest disappeared.

The next day, the guest appeared to the synagogue caretaker in a dream and revealed that he was Abraham. He had seen the sorrow of his children and came to complete their quorum. Since then, the synagogue has been called the Avraham Avinu (Abraham our Father) Synagogue.

For centuries, the Avraham Avinu Synagogue was the spiritual center of the Sephardic Jewish community in

Hebron. The community members and their leaders prayed there, among them famous Kabbalists whose books were disseminated from Hebron to the entire Jewish world. These Kabbalists include the authors of the books *Chesed L'Avraham*, *Melechet Shlomo* and *Reishit Chochmah*, who all lived in Hebron in the 16th century.

Ya'akov Hayyim Castel and Chacham David Agababa, leaders of the Sephardic community, at the entrance of the Jewish Quarter (the Ghetto), 1921 Credit Ya'acov Ben-Dov

In the Torah ark, the treasure of the community has been preserved – antique, precious Torah scrolls brought to Hebron throughout the generations. With the conquest of Gaza by Napoleon in 1799, the Gazan Jews fled to Hebron, bringing their Torah ark and Torah scrolls with them. This ornate ark, sculpted from sycamore trees, was set at the right of the Avraham Avinu Synagogue interior. Forty years later, the doors of the Gaza synagogue, embedded with seashells, were also brought to Hebron and installed at a side entrance to the synagogue. These doors were burned after the Jewish community was expelled.

Carved wooden doors originally taken from the Gaza synagogue and reinstalled in the Avraham Avinu synagogue. Photo credit: Jacob Pinkerfeld, 1936

The Torah ark

*Torah scrolls desecrated in the 1929 riots
Credit: Gabi Kadmon*

The 1929 Massacre and the Destruction of the Jewish Quarter

Arab marauders attacked the Jewish Quarter in the 1929 (5689) massacre, murdered Jewish residents, and ransacked and defiled the Avraham Avinu synagogue. Jewish community members managed to save the ancient Torah scrolls at great risk to their lives. The British police expelled the survivors of the massacre to Jerusalem, where they established a synagogue called *Ohel Avraham* (Tent of Abraham) and preserved the rare Torah scrolls. The destruction of the Avraham Avinu synagogue began a number of years later, still during the British Mandate. During the Jordanian occupation (1948 - 1967) the entire Jewish quarter was destroyed. An animal pen was built on the remains of the Avraham Avinu synagogue and next to it a public latrine was constructed. The entire surroundings of the synagogue were covered with ruins and refuse and exuded an unpleasant odor.

The ruins of the Jewish Quarter

The Arab marketplace on the ruins of the Jewish Quarter

The public latrine next to the ruins of the Avraham Avinu Synagogue

The Avraham Avinu Synagogue following the 1929 massacre (credit: US Library of Congress archives)

The destroyed Jewish Quarter following the Jordanian occupation

The Avraham Avinu Synagogue reduced to an animal pen

Animal pen on the ruins of the synagogue

Following a lengthy public battle, the Israeli government authorized the uncovering of the Avraham Avinu synagogue in 1976 (5736). With concentrated effort, the remains of the building were unearthed. Later, the Israeli government authorized the rebuilding and restoration of the synagogue.

The Avraham Avinu synagogue in ruin and during the work to uncover it

Among the diggers: Eliezer Breuer and Shmuel Mushnick (left), Noam Arnon (right)

The Avraham Avinu Synagogue during restoration

The Avraham Avinu Synagogue was restored by architect Dan Tanai according to floor plans and photographs of the original synagogue. The same architect also restored synagogues in the Jewish Quarter in Jerusalem. The original marble floor of the synagogue was replicated using flooring brought from the old Shaare Zedek hospital in Jerusalem.

When we open the doors of the Torah ark in the Avraham Avinu synagogue, we can see antique Torah scrolls that bear special significance. These Torah scrolls were the treasure of the old Jewish community of Hebron. During the 1929 massacre, a number of young members of the Jewish community risked their lives to rescue some of the Torah scrolls, which they carried with them when they were expelled from their hometown. These Torah scrolls were preserved by the Committee of Hebron Refugees in the Ohel Avraham synagogue in Jerusalem, anticipating their return to Hebron. Nobody knew if and when that would take place. The dream was fulfilled in 1967 (5727), when Hebron was liberated and a major effort was made to restore the community and redeem the Jewish Quarter.

Following the completion of the synagogue restoration in 1981 (5741), the Torah scrolls rescued during the massacre were returned to the Avraham Avinu synagogue in a festive, moving ceremony. Representatives of the Sephardic community, among them survivors of the massacre, had the unique privilege of placing the Torah scrolls back into the ark from which they had been previously removed.

Today, daily prayers ascend from the restored synagogue, serving as an active spiritual center for the community. Part of the Jewish Quarter surrounding the synagogue has been rebuilt. Jewish homes, kindergartens, and the Eshel Avraham (Oak of Abraham) guesthouse are part of the now-flourishing neighborhood.

The Chabad Synagogue

There is another small synagogue behind the Avraham Avinu synagogue which is called by several names: the Mitteler Rebbe Synagogue, the Menucha Rachel Synagogue, or the Ashkenazic Avraham Avinu synagogue. It is located in a side section that was purchased in 1817 (5577) by Chabad emissary Shimon Shmerling, marking the beginning of the Chabad community in Hebron. The Mitteler Rebbe, the second leader of the Chabad movement (1773 - 1827), encouraged his hasidim to make aliyah to Hebron and to buy land there. His hasidim and later his daughter, Menucha Rachel, and her husband, Rabbi Yaakov Slonim, and her family made aliyah to Hebron and established a prominent Chabad community there. This small synagogue, along with the entire Jewish quarter, was destroyed under Jordanian rule. It was rediscovered after the return to Hebron. The building was restored in a unique manner by the stone artist Eliyahu Idinov. It was dedicated in 2005 (5765).

At the synagogue entrance is a display of photographs and documents, some of them handwritten, and some of the original objects that belonged to the Chabad Jewish community in Hebron.

Beit Romano

Let us continue down King David Street. In just a few minutes, we will reach the Hezekiah - Nachalat Chabad neighborhood.

Beit Romano is the focal point of the neighborhood and houses the Shavei Hevron yeshiva. Construction for the new Hezekiah - Nachalat Chabad neighborhood began in 2020.

In 1871 (5631), Chaim Yisrael Romano of Istanbul purchased a large plot of land outside the Jewish quarter of Hebron. In 1876 (5636), he built Beit Romano in the center of the neighborhood. Beit Romano was a grand, three-story building called "the palace." It was used for living quarters, a study hall, and an old-age home for elderly Jews who came to Hebron from Turkey. In 1888 (5648), an additional section was added to the building upon the initiative of the Charif, Rabbi Chaim Rachamim Yosef Franko. A Jewish neighborhood, made up of businessmen, slowly developed to the building's south.

At the beginning of the 20th century, Rabbi Chaim Hezekiah Medini, author of the great Talmudic encyclopedia *Sde Chemed*, made aliyah to Hebron. He lived in the home of the Charif and housed his extensive library there. His study hall was established in the adjacent Beit Romano. In 1905 (5766), Avraham Romano, the son of Chaim Yisrael Romano and inheritor of the building, planned to sell the large plot to a wealthy Arab resident of Hebron who had known his father. Rabbi Shimon Hausman, a central figure in the adjacent neighborhood, quickly purchased the plot, enlisting the financial help of the fifth Lubavitcher Rebbe, Rabbi Sholom Dovber Schneersohn (the Rebbe Rashab). In 1912 (5672), the Rebbe Rashab purchased the building and the surrounding courtyard and established the Toras Emes yeshiva there. The yeshiva was geared for a select group of Chabad youth who came from Russia to learn there.

The Chabad hasidim were expelled from the Land of Israel during World War I, and the building was expropriated by the Turkish army. After the British triumph, the building was not returned to its owners and the British police were housed there. It was the British police who turned their backs on the security of the Jews in Hebron during the massacre in 1929.

Restoration of the Istanbuli synagogue

A large mob of Arab residents attacked the Jewish community in Hebron, murdering 67 Jews, injuring and maiming unarmed civilians, raping women and burning homes. Two of the wounded later died of their injuries. The Jewish survivors were gathered in the police station in Beit Romano.

The British police gathered the Arab perpetrators on the ground floor, later freeing most of them. The remnants of the Jewish community were expelled from Hebron and their homes were looted.

Following the Jordanian occupation in 1948, a school was established in Beit Romano. In 1982, the building was returned to the Jewish community of Hebron with the authorization and support of the Lubavitcher Rebbe, leader of Chabad, which owned the building. Initially, the building housed families. Later, Yeshivat Shavei Hevron was established there. Today, the yeshiva is flourishing, with approximately 300 students. A new study hall was built on top of the original building. It serves as an educational campus and architectural gem in the developing Jewish community of Hebron. The building also houses a restoration of the original unique synagogue of the Istanbul Jewish community.

Beit Romano: The original structure and the added floors

Hezekiah Quarter – Nachalat Chabad

Beit Romano and the adjacent lot were purchased by Chabad more than 100 years ago. Even after the expulsion of the Jews following the massacre of 1929, the Lubavitcher Rebbe continued to preserve the movement's rights to the plot. The Jordanians wanted to expropriate the Jewish properties in Hebron, which it defined as "the property of the Zionist enemy." The Jordanian government utilized the Jewish properties for their municipality. A marketplace and garbage dump were built on the ruins of the Jewish quarter, and a bus station was built in the southern section of Nachalat Chabad.

These additions to the old section of the city created crowding, traffic and public health impediments. Hence, during the 1980s and 1990s, they were transferred to their permanent location adjacent to the central road in western Hebron. This transfer cleared space for the Jewish properties and made it possible for Jewish families to live there in temporary dwellings. An IDF army base was also established there in temporary buildings.

At the beginning of the 2000s, plans were laid for the construction of permanent housing on the property, called the Hezekiah Quarter–Nachalat Chabad. Due to legal delays, the plans took a long time to prepare. In 2020 - 2022, a permanent replacement building was constructed for the army base. The foundations were dug for the apartment buildings planned to house 30 apartments and educational institutions.

Artist's rendition of Hezekiah Quarter - Nachalat Chabad neighborhood

Beit Hadassah

The Jewish community of Hebron began building Beit Hadassah in 1893 (5653) as the Chesed L'Avraham clinic and hospital. It serviced all the residents of the city.

Beit Hadassah as it appears today, with both the original structure and the additions

Many of the donors for the building were members of the Jewish communities of Algiers, who were enlisted by

Rabbi Chaim Rachamim Yosef Franko of Hebron (the Charif). Initially, two floors of the building were constructed, with an ornate façade facing the street to the north. Today, Jews do not have access to that street. The building was called Chesed L'Avraham (Kindness of Abraham).

At the beginning of the 20th century, an additional floor was added to the building, with contributions from the philanthropist Yosef Avraham Shalom of India. He was memorialized in an engraving on the façade of the building. The Sasson family of India contributed as well. The hospital operated until World War I. Later, the American-founded Hadassah organization opened a clinic at the building and from that time on, it was called Beit Hadassah. Jewish families with members employed at the hospital and community leadership lived in the adjacent homes, among them the families of Rabbi Chanoch Hasson, Rabbi Shmuel Castel, the leaders of the Sephardic community, and the family of the pharmacist Ben Tzion Gershon. To the east of Beit Hadassah stood a large guest house operated by the Ashkenazic Chabad community. It was established and run by the Kazarnovsky–Schneerson family and still bears their name today as Beit Schneerson.

In the past, there had been friendly, neighborly relations between Jews and Arabs in Hebron. This era came to a screeching halt with a horrifying event, the massacre of 1929 (5689). Riots against Jewish communities throughout Israel were initiated by Haj Amin al-Husseini, a leader of the Arab-Muslim community and later a Nazi collaborator. Over 130 Jews were murdered. The mobs attacked Jews throughout Israel, from Haifa and Tzfat in the north to Be'er Tuvia and Hulda in the south, as well as Jerusalem and Tel Aviv. In Hebron, 67 Jews were slaughtered and numerous were wounded, two of whom later died of their injuries. Most of the families living in the Beit Hadassah area were severely injured in the 1929 massacre, many of them murdered with unfathomable cruelty. The survivors were removed from the city and their possessions were looted.

The northern side of Beit Hadassah. Following the Jordanian occupation, the original ornate entrance became a store.

The Beit Hadassah clinic after the massacre. Credit: Central Zionist Archives.

A British policeman at the entrance to Beit Hadassah after the massacre

Upper right: Amin al-Husseini meeting with Nazi leader Adolf Hitler (Credit: 1941, German Federal Archives). Upper left: Al-Husseini recruiting Bosnian Muslims to join the Nazis. (Credit: 1943, German Federal Archives). Lower left: prayer books desecrated, Hebron 1929. Lower right: survivor of 1929 Hebron massacre at British police station

Fifty years later, in 1979, Jews returned to permanently settle in Hebron. At the beginning, they lived in Beit Hadassah, which had stood empty and abandoned, waiting to be redeemed. A group of women and children entered the building in the middle of the night and announced: We have returned home to the city of the Patriarchs and Matriarchs to rebuild its Jewish community!

Children returning to Beit Hadassah in 1979

Supply line to the pioneering women in Beit Hadassah, 1979

They determinedly remained in Beit Hadassah despite living in very difficult conditions, without electricity or working plumbing. They were in a state of siege, with no one allowed in or out. Their husbands and fathers were not allowed into the building. Nonetheless, the mothers and children tenaciously persevered with devotion and faith.

Approximately a year later, Friday night, May 2, 1980 (17th of Iyar 5740), a terrorist cell waited in ambush outside of Beit Hadassah. The terrorists knew the husbands and fathers of the women and children inside the building, joined by Nir Yeshiva students, would be gathering to make the *Kiddush* ceremony. As the group approached the building, the terrorists opened gunfire and threw grenades. Six Jews were murdered and twenty were wounded in the attack. Yet the terrorists achieved the opposite of their goal. In response to the attack, the government of Israel decided to officially renew the Jewish presence in Hebron.

Rebbetzin Miriam Levinger, the driving force behind the women of Beit Hadassah. Her husband, Rabbi Moshe Levinger is on the other side of the gate.

Beit Hadassah was restored by renowned architect David Cassuto. Two additional floors were added to the building while preserving its original façade. He used the original stone masonry to fashion the upper window gables, which are similar to the original gables on the lower windows. In addition, a large window of Stars of David made of cement was built on the upper-level façade, making Beit Hadassah a unique architectural gem.

Today, the upper floors of Beit Hadassah serve as residential apartments while the ground floor houses the Hebron Heritage Museum. One of the highlights of the museum is a multimedia presentation that tells the story of the Jewish community in Hebron throughout the generations. The museum also features a cafeteria and gift shop. (More information at the end of this booklet).

Exhibits in the Hebron Heritage Museum

The memory of the six young men murdered in the Beit Hadassah terrorist attack of 1980 is memorialized in Beit Hashishah (The House of the Six), a modern apartment building built in 2000 in response to the murderous attack that aimed to uproot the Jews from Hebron.

Across the street from Beit Hashishah is a grassy seating

area for tour groups. It was built in honor of the visit of Israeli President Reuven Rivlin at the dedication of the Hebron Heritage Museum in 2015 (5775).

From Beit Hadassah we will go up to the Biblical Tel Hebron. We can ascend on a picturesque trail that begins with the stairs across from Beit Hadassah, or follow the paved road that continues straight and then turns left up a steep hill. At the intersection at the top of the hill, turn left to the Jewish neighborhood called Admot Yishai.

Children in the Beit Hadassah playground

Tel Hebron - The Site of Biblical Hebron

Tel Hebron sits on a broad, picturesque hill overlooking the Hebron Valley. This is the site of Biblical Hebron. The Bible relates many details about Hebron during the era of the Patriarchs and Matriarchs (3,500 - 4,000 years ago) and about Hebron as a fortress city when the scouts came to investigate the Land of Israel (approximately 3,300 years ago). The Book of Samuel mentions Hebron during the era of the Davidic monarchy as a walled city in Judea (3,000 years ago). Impressive Jewish remains were discovered there from 2,000 years ago as well as even older pre-Israelite remains. A visit to Tel Hebron is an experience that combines history, Bible, archeology, nature, and even current events.

Today, the Admot Yishai neighborhood shares space with amazing archeological sites. At the entrance to the neighborhood, we can see the wall of the city from the early Bronze Age. The wall was built approximately 4,500 years ago. Next to it is another wall from the middle Bronze Age (the era of the Patriarchs and Matriarchs). Between the two walls we can see a staircase that led to the city gate, preserved in excellent condition.

It can be surmised that this was the gate where Abraham and Efron the Hittite negotiated during the purchase of the Cave of Machpelah. The wall is part of the fortifications that surrounded the ancient city. Its width is approximately 6.5 meters, and in the past, its height was approximately 10 meters. We will pass the wall and enter the ancient city.

The most visible finding is the ruins of a four-room house, a Jewish home from the ancient Israelite period (the Iron Age, 10th - 8th centuries BCE.) A number of seals upon which were embossed the words "[Belonging] to the king, Hebron" (LMLK seals) were found in the house. The seals were written in ancient Hebrew script used in the time of King Hezekiah (8th century BCE). The seals were common throughout the Judean kingdom. They were embossed on the handles of jugs that contained agricultural produce (wine, oil and more) and were stored in the royal warehouses. The seals all said "To (meaning 'belonging to') the king" with the name of one of the four cities in the inheritance of the tribe of Judea: Hebron, Socho, Zif and Mameshet. Hundreds of seals were discovered at various archeological sites in Judea. The vast dissemination of the "to the king, Hebron" seals testifies to the central place of Hebron in Judea during the First Temple era.

 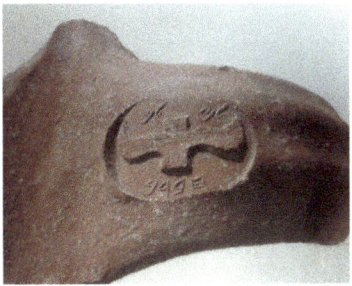

"To the king, Hebron" seal with two wings from the era of King Hezekiah, king of Judea. Credit: Land of Judea Museum / Prof. Boaz Zissu

"To the king, Hebron" seal, with four wings

On the back wall of the site we can see murals by Israeli artist Solomon Souza that depict life in the ancient city. In the painting we can see the gate to the city and the famous event that took place there, the transfer of the silver from Abraham to Ephron to purchase the Cave of Machpelah. Also depicted is an ancient Jewish farmer with sheaves he has harvested, as well as King David as king in Hebron with people pressing wine in the winepress discovered here.

The remains of an Israelite Four-Room House. Murals by artist Solomon Souza depict ancient Jewish life in Hebron.

The wall and stairs from the Early Bronze Era

Decorated bowl, late Bronze era, discovered in Tel Hebron. Credit: Land of Judea Museum

Tel Hebron includes several sites:
- The Admot Yishai Jewish neighborhood
- The Biblical Hebron site
- Rooftop observation
- Tomb of Yishai (Jesse) and Ruth
- Abraham's Spring
- Canaanite Walls
- Ancient olive trees
- Ancient Tel Hebron archeological site

Admot Yishai Neighborhood

Most of the Tel Hebron area was purchased by the Jewish community of Hebron 200 years ago. The area included ancient olive trees, referred to in the deeds as "the olives of the Jews." According to the agreement between the Jewish community and the Arab community that lived nearby, the Arabs would harvest the olives, produce olive oil and receive part of the oil as their payment. After the 1929 massacre, the expulsion of the Jews, and the Jordanian occupation in 1948 (5708), Arab residents appropriated parts of the territory and conducted illegal and damaging construction at the archeological site.

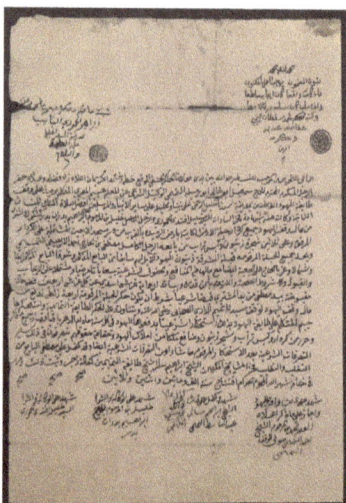

Deeds of the Jewish land purchases in Tel Hebron from the early 1800s.

Site map:
1. Canaanite wall
2. Glacis (slope)
3. Wall from the seventh century BCE
4. The Stepped Street
5. Eastern ritual bath
6. Western ritual bath
7-8 Winepress treading floor Cisterns
9. Remains of an olive press collecting vat.
10. Pools for filtering clay
11. Pool of a workshop for manufacturing pottery vessels
12. Pottery kiln
13. The Burnt Room

Aerial photograph of Tel Hebron. Credit: Dr. Gershon Bar-Cochva

Following the liberation of Hebron in 1967 (5727), the deeds for the Jewish land were re-examined, and the Jewish ownership of the land on Tel Hebron was verified. In 1984 (5744) a plan for a Jewish neighborhood in part of the area was authorized and the Jewish neighborhood of Admot Yishai was established. The neighborhood consisted of seven trailer homes (caravans). The residents lived in difficult conditions and were somewhat isolated from the other Jewish neighborhoods in Hebron.

Beit Menachem

In 1998 (5758) an Arab terrorist infiltrated the Admot Yishai neighborhood and brutally murdered Rabbi Shlomo Ra'anan in his home. On the heels of the attack, the Israeli government authorized the construction of the Beit Menachem apartment building, which would afford a sense of permanency and greater protection for the residents of the neighborhood.

In preparation for the building, archeological excavations were conducted in 1999 which revealed unique artifacts (to be discussed below). After the preservation of these artifacts, the Beit Menachem building was constructed on pillars to preserve the archeological finds below. The building was dedicated in 2005. In addition to Beit Menachem, another plot of land was purchased. Today, the Admot Yishai neighborhood includes Beit Menachem, several homes and the Dagan Garden to the east, where one can enjoy the panoramic view of the valley of the old city of Hebron below.

The Four-Room House

Wine presses from the Talmudic era were discovered near the Four-Room House. After the excavation and preservation were completed, Beit Menachem was constructed on pillars to preserve the archeological findings.

This building is a living example of the essence of the Jewish community in Hebron: A modern community whose foundations rest upon more than 4,000 years of history.

The Rooftop Observation Point – Beit Menachem

From atop Beit Menachem we can see a panoramic view of Hebron and its surroundings.

To the south, we can see Tel Hebron and at its center, the ancient structure atop the Tomb of Jesse and Ruth.

The more distant mountain range is Abu Sneineh, which overlooks Hebron from the south. At the top of the mountains is an army base that was established after terrorists of the Second Intifada began shooting at the Jewish community, resulting in the murder of baby Shalhevet Pas from sniper fire in 2001. To the southeast we can see the edge of the Judean Desert. On a clear day, we can see the Moab Mountains in Jordan.

To our west, we can see the ancient Jewish cemetery and at its center, the plot for the victims of the 1929 massacre. There is also a small military plot. At the foot of the mountain range we see the road to Beersheba and the peaks of the western mountains that overlook the Mediterranean shore.

Hebron 1967: A small town (Photo: Alex Libak)

To the east we can see the Hebron Valley, with the Tomb of the Patriarchs and Matriarchs at its center. Above the original Jewish structure, we can clearly see the additions added later: the roof of the Crusader church and the minarets of the mosques from the Mamluk era.

The Hebron Valley is mentioned in the Bible when Jacob sends Joseph to his brothers in Shechem (Genesis 37:14). Today, the Hebron Valley is mostly filled with buildings from the Middle Ages, after the ancient city of Tel Hebron was destroyed and the city grew into the valley. In the past, this valley was filled with fields, and the Cave of Machpelah was at the edge of the field, as described in Genesis chapter 23. In the heart of the Hebron Valley, we can see the Jewish Quarter, at the center of which is the Avraham Avinu synagogue. Near the Jewish quarter, we can see Beit Romano. Above the Tomb of the Patriarchs and Matriarchs, in the midst of a patch of trees, we see Kiryat Arba, the Jewish town adjacent to Hebron, which was established in 1971 (5731). Above Kiryat Arba we see the antennas of the army outpost on Gal Hill.

Looking north, we see the Nimra mountain range. The name is believed to come from the Biblical name Mamre, one of the ancient names of Hebron. According to tradition, Abraham sat under oak trees on this hill, where he welcomed the three angels and received the promise of the imminent birth of his son, Isaac (Genesis 13:18).

To the west, we see the new section of Hebron, a city with a modern, flourishing and vibrant economy. We can see shopping centers, malls and office buildings. Hebron is built on approximately 22,000 dunam (22 square kilometers), roughly the size of the Israeli cities of Rehovot or Holon, and has a population of 200,000. The city boasts approximately 20,000 businesses, factories and stores. The industry in Hebron is closely connected to the Israeli market. Billions of shekels of merchandise manufactured in Hebron annually make their way to Israeli markets.

Left: Hebron in the early 1970s shortly after its liberation. Prior to this, the city resembled a small town with a quaint, old-time atmosphere. Right: Post-liberation, Hebron experienced rapid economic growth and swift development, transforming into a thriving, modern city.

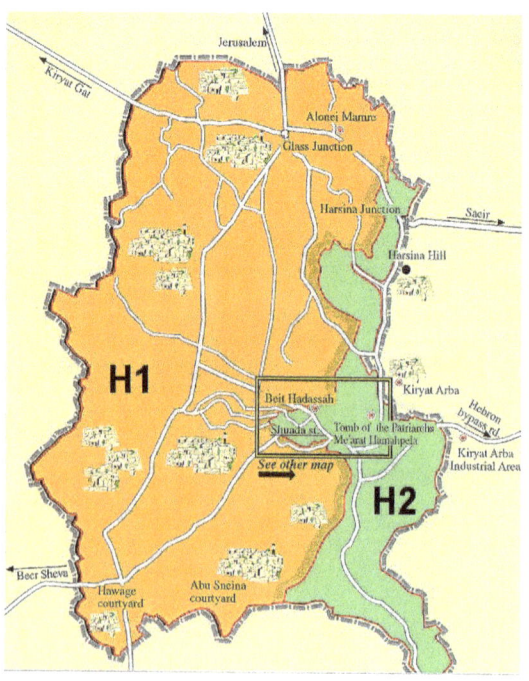

The map of Hebron today. Jews are allowed only in the green area

This part of the city is where the Knesset Yisrael (Slabodka) yeshiva once existed when its faculty and students made aliyah to Hebron from Slabodka, Lithuania, in 1924. The yeshiva flourished in Hebron until the 1929 massacre when 20 students were murdered. Following the massacre, the yeshiva moved to Jerusalem. Its name became Yeshivat Hevron (the Hebron Yeshiva) which it still retains today.

Knesset Yisrael Yeshiva in Hebron, 1928

Knesset Yisrael Yeshiva in Hebron, 1996, before it was demolished by the Palestinian Authority

In the past, Jews could visit, shop and walk throughout Hebron. In 1997 (5757), the city was divided under the Hebron Accords and Jews were restricted to only Jewish neighborhoods regardless of their citizenship status. Only 3% of the city is open to Jews.

The Tomb of Yishai (Jesse) and Ruth

At the high point of Tel Hebron, there is an ancient structure which, according to early tradition, is identified as the Tomb of Yishai (Jesse) and Ruth. Some scholars believe this was the location of King David's original palace. Since the Middle Ages, this site and the Crusader structure atop it, have been called the Tomb of Yishai. Later, a tradition developed according to which Ruth, King David's great-grandmother, was also buried here. This site was considered holy to Jews throughout the generations and became a traditional place of prayer.

From the top of the structure, there is an observation point where one can see the Hebron Valley to the east, as well as the southern and western parts of the city. Researchers believe the building next to the main structure was an ancient Byzantine synagogue. The site has been recently restored and the well-kept garden areas provide a place for a pleasant atmosphere for groups and visitors.

The Eastern Trail

From the Tomb of Jesse and Ruth (as well as from Dagan Garden), we can walk on a path that encircles Tel Hebron from the east. This trail connects several interesting sites – the Tomb of Jesse and Ruth, Dagan Garden, Abraham's Spring, Beit Hadassah, ancient olive trees and ancient Tel

Hebron. We can also descend from the trail to the Hebron Valley, the Jewish Quarter and the Tomb of the Patriarchs and Matriarchs. In springtime, wild flowers bloom along the path, giving it the feel of a nature trail.

The residents of Admot Yishai dedicated the Dagan Garden in memory of IDF Officer Dagan Wertman, who served in Hebron as a platoon commander in the Golani Brigade and fell in Operation Cast Lead in Gaza in 2009 (5769). The observation point there was built in memory of Yona Haikin, a resident of Hebron who passed away in 1991 (5752).

Abraham's Spring

This spring was the city's first water source and one of the contributing factors to the building of Hebron at this site. It is called Abraham's Spring to illustrate its antiquity. It was originally outside the city walls, but it is possible that there was a connection between the spring and the inside of the city. In excavations above the spring, layers of the city of Hebron from the Canaanite era through the Byzantine era were discovered. Originally, there was an open pool here. It is possible that this was the location where the murderers of Ish-bosheth, the son of King Saul, were executed, as it is written: "And David commanded the young men, and they killed them… and they hanged them by the pool in Hebron." (II Samuel 4:12). During the Second Temple era, stairs were carved from the rock, similar to mikvahs (ritual pools) from that era.

Hebron was destroyed after the Byzantine era. When the Arabs came to Hebron in 638, the city was found burned and in ruins. According to several opinions, this is the source of the Arabic name for the site, Tel Rumeida, which means ash. The spring was covered with layers of soil. After it was unearthed in the Middle Ages, it was called Ein Jedidah, which means "the new spring," even though the spring existed even before the city had been established. A wall surrounds the spring and steep stairs lead down to the water. In the 1980s, the inner space of the spring was cleaned and a carved pool approximately eight meters deep was discovered.

In recent years, the spring has once again become a point of interest. It was cleaned and repaired and a cement wall was built around it. With the renewal of the Jewish community in Hebron, Jews began to recite the Rosh Hashanah *Tashlich* prayer at the spring. The site is easily accessible and just a few minutes from the Jewish quarter, Abraham Avinu neighborhood, Shavei Hevron yeshiva and Beit Hadassah. A bus stop can be found at the foot of the hill leading to the spring. Many take advantage of its cold water for a purifying and refreshing immersion, particularly before Shabbat and festivals and during the summer. Paths from the spring lead to the ancient olive trees on Tel Hebron, the Cannanite Wall, the Admot Yishai neighborhood, and the Tomb of Jesse and Ruth. A visit to the spring can be included in a fascinating tour of these sites.

Canaanite Wall / Wall of the Giants

Remnants of walls built around Tel Hebron still exist at the site. The walls are impressive in their magnitude, width, the size of the rocks and the strength of the fortification they created. The discovery of the wall dovetails with Biblical references to the giants said to have lived in Hebron in ancient times (Numbers 13:22, 28; Deuteronomy 1:28; Joshua 14:12 and more) and was hence called the "Wall of Giants." According to the Biblical account (Numbers 13) the magnitude of the walls surrounding Hebron was of great concern to Israel's leaders, who were sent by Moses on a mission to scout the land before the Israelites were to enter. Only Joshua and Caleb remained faithful to the mission and the Land of Israel. As a result, they were granted the privilege of entering and inheriting the land.

According to the Midrash on the verse, "and they ascended in the Negev and he came until Hebron" (Numbers 13:22) Caleb's courage was the result of his prayer at the burial site of the Patriarchs and Matriarchs in the Cave of Machpelah.

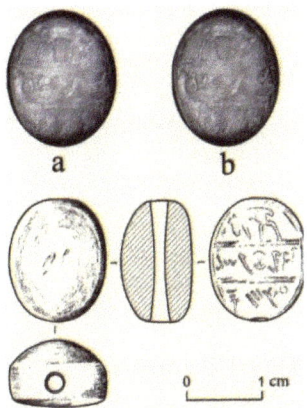

Hebrew seal with the words "To Shfatyahu ben Samach" discovered at Tel Hebron

These walls were built in the mid-Bronze era – parallel to the era of the Patriarchs and Matriarchs (approximately 3,800 years ago). During the era of the kingdom of Judea, a watchtower and slanted wall were added, improving the fortification's defensive capabilities. The walls were in use during the Canaanite and Israelite eras, until the end of the First Temple era, when the kingdom of Judea fell to the kingdom of Babylonia (586 BCE). A large portion of the southern wall line was revealed in excavations. Written findings from the Israelite era were found near the wall – a seal and an ostracon (pottery fragment with writing) with names ending in the typical Jewish suffix of the time, "yahu."

Ancient Olive Trees

In the upper central section of Tel Hebron, we see ancient, picturesque olive trees. They can be accessed via the eastern trail. Some of these trees are hundreds of years old and possibly even older. Experts believe that some trees may be 1,500 years old, meaning they were planted during the Byzantine era when the Tel was not settled. The trees are exposed to various pests and need constant care to safeguard this natural historical treasure.

The Cannanite Wall and the ancient olive trees in Tel Hebron

The Canaanite Wall and a tower from the Israelite era

Ancient Tel Hebron Archeological Site

A Canaanite tablet from the era of the Forefathers and Mothers was discovered in Tel Hebron. The document, written on a clay tablet in the Akkadian language, includes a list of animals and offerings that were brought for sacrifice and for the king.

The excavations in Tel Hebron were conducted in the lots bought by the Jewish community 200 years ago. Fortunately, these lots were open, making it possible to dig there. In 2014 (5774), archaeologists Professor David Ben Shlomo from Ariel University and Professor Emanuel Eisenberg from the Israel Antiquities Authority excavated the site. They discovered surprising and important historical artifacts from the Second Temple Era (2,000 years ago, from the 1st century BCE to the 1st century CE). The primary discovery was a neighborhood of residential houses and an industrial area of Jewish Hebron from the Roman era.

On the north side of the area, a workshop for pottery vessels was discovered. Next to it are two giant public mikvahs (ritual baths), among the largest mikvahs ever discovered. The volume of one of the mikvahs is 100 cubic meters, and the volume of the second is over 200 cubic meters. An interesting aspect of the discovery is that these mikvahs had a separation between the stairs leading down into the mikvah and the stairs upon which the newly purified people ascended from immersion. Next to the mikvahs, wine presses and a winery were discovered, and oil presses were uncovered nearby. These discoveries reveal a tangible picture of Jewish Hebron during the Second Temple Era.

The Jews of ancient Hebron were rigorous about purity and manufactured pure wine that was sent to Jerusalem for pilgrims coming to the Temple. These findings dovetail beautifully with the Mishnah in *Hagigah* 3:4: "In Judea, they are trusted as to the purity of the wine and oil all days of the year, during the period of the wine press and olive oil press, they are trusted on the purity of *terumah*, as well." We can imagine the ancient Jewish workers arriving at Tel Hebron every morning, immersing in the mikvahs and continuing together to their work, creating pottery vessels or pressing wine or oil.

The archeological findings clearly show that the residents of ancient Hebron were Jews. This negates the claims of some researchers who hypothesized that the Edomites lived in Hebron at that time.

The two mikvahs in Tel Hebron are among the largest discovered from the Second Temple Era.

Historic sources relate that the Edomites converted to Judaism in the Hasmonean era (end of 2nd century BCE) and even had an active role in the Great Jewish Revolt against the Romans. Jewish Hebron was destroyed by the Romans during the rebellion (67 - 70 CE). In the dig, a room was discovered with household items that had been smashed, burned, and then repaired. The Jewish community in the city was renewed and then participated in the Bar Kochba Revolt (132 - 135 CE). A silver dinar from the days of Bar Kochba was also discovered in the excavations.

A silver dinar from the days of the Bar Kochba Revolt discovered at Tel Hebron

Following the Bar Kochba Revolt, Jews were prohibited from living in Judea and the community of Tel Hebron was abandoned. However, Jews continued to come to Hebron to pray at the Tomb of the Patriarchs and Matriarchs. The Jewish community in Hebron was renewed in the early Arabic Era, in the Jewish quarter adjacent to the Tomb of the Patriarchs and Matriarchs.

Tel Hebron is maintained and operated by the Nature and Parks Authority. Information on guided tours can be obtained from en.parks.org.il. During the Holidays – *Chol Hamoed* Succot and Pesach, shuttles from the Tomb of the Patriarchs and Matriarchs to Tel Hebron are operated by the Jewish Community of Hebron.

Ways to get there:

Walking: Take the eastern or western trails.

By vehicle: Take the road ascending from the Jewish cemetery. Guards will open the gate for vehicles upon request. Entry is free and the site is open every day. On Thursdays and Fridays, a guide from the Nature and Parks Authority is at the site.

Ancient Hebron (Artwork by Shalom Kweller)

The Western Trail

From the ancient Tel Hebron site we can return to the Admot Yishai neighborhood on the western trail. Along the trail we see a trench that was the base of the western wall of the city. The ditch was necessary because, from this direction, the Tel is topographically connected to the mountain range to the west, requiring additional fortification on this side. From this trail we can see the new city and the ancient Jewish cemetery to our west. It is near this trail that in 1988, archeologist Yuval Peleg discovered a grave with a wealth of artifacts from the Late Bronze (Canaanite) Age, parallel to the era of Joshua ben Nun and the beginning of the Israelite inheritance of the Land of Israel.

Photo of Ma'ale Yuval trail

The Ancient Cemetery

The ancient Jewish cemetery in Hebron is approximately 1,000 years old and contains an estimated 5,000 graves. Most of the cemetery was destroyed during the Jordanian occupation between 1948 and 1967. Following the liberation of Hebron, part of the cemetery was reconstructed. Today, it serves as the burial place for Kiryat Arba and Hebron residents.

Burial in the cemetery was reinstated in 1975 after the tragic death of baby Avraham Yedidya Nachshon. His mother, Sarah Nachshon, fought for the right to bury her son in the cemetery. Later, the broken pieces of the headstones of the victims of the 1929 massacre were discovered nearby by Professor Ben Tzion Tavger. This discovery made it possible to reconstruct the headstones of the victims, who were buried in a common grave.

Professor Ben Tzion Tavger. Credit: Gershon Elinson

The broken headstones of the victims of the 1929 massacre

The original cemetery was divided into four parts. The southern (upper) portion consists of ancient plots. To the east is the Karaite section, and to the west is the rabbinical section. Most of this area was not damaged and the original gravestones can be seen. The rest of the sections of the cemetery were severely damaged during the Jordanian occupation.

The graves of the victims of the 1929 massacre. Credit: Y. Goldman collection

The cemetery in 1931. Credit: Y. Alexandroni collection

At the edge of the path to the left of the entrance gate is the section of the rabbis and Kabbalists of the Sephardic community. There used to be a custom in Hebron not to write names or inscriptions on the gravestones, therefore, most of the graves remain unidentified. In this section, one grave that stands out is that of the famous author of the kabbalistic book *Reisheet Chochmah*, Rabbi Eliyahu De Vidas (died 1587). A large tombstone was built over his grave in the 18th century. It was destroyed after the 1929 massacre and reconstructed after the liberation of Hebron. Next to him is the grave of Rabbi Chaim Hezekiyah Medini (died 1904), chief rabbi of Hebron and author of the multi-volume Talmudic encyclopedia Sde Chemed.

The graves of the Reisheet Chochmah and the Sde Chemed

Other important rabbis buried here include Rabbi Shlomo Adani (1567 - circa 1630), author of the comprehensive commentary on the Mishnah, *Melechet Shlomo*. The graves of the Chief Rabbi of Hebron, Rabbi Eliyahu Mani, and his wife Samra are easily recognizable by their different direction. In his will, Rabbi Mani stated he wished to be buried in the direction of the Tomb of the Patriarchs and Matriarchs and not toward Jerusalem, as per the usual tradition. His son, Rabbi Suleiman Menachem Mani, born in 1850, who succeeded his father as rabbi of Hebron, was also buried here in 1924 (5684). In 2015 (5775), Rabbi Moshe Levinger, founder of the renewed Jewish community of Hebron, was buried here. At the top of the cemetery, the monument built over the grave of Rabbi Avraham Azulai (1570-1643), author of the *Chesed L'Avraham*, stands out. Rabbi Azulai was one of the great sages of Israel. According to legend, he passed away after entering the depths of the Cave of Machpelah.

Across from the entrance to the cemetery, we see the gravesite for the Torah scrolls that were desecrated in the Tomb of the Patriarchs and Matriarchs on Yom Kippur Eve 1976 (5737).

On the right-hand side of the entrance gate is the section of the victims of the 1929 massacre, four rows, with a total of 60 graves. The other victims were buried in other cities. This section was desecrated and destroyed in a most horrifying manner during the Jordanian occupation. It was reconstructed 50 years after the massacre in 1979 (5739).

Next is a small military section with three graves: Eli Haze'ev, who fell in the Beit Hadassah terrorist attack in 1980 (5740), Staff Sergeant Elazar Lebovitch, who fell in a terrorist attack in 2002 (5762), and Major Benaya Sarel, who fell in Operation Protective Edge in 2014 (5774).

To the right of the 1929 massacre victims section is the grave of Avraham Yedidyah Nachshon, a baby who tragically died in 1975. Inscribed on his tombstone is the unique story of his mother's courage in holding his funeral in the cemetery despite opposition, making it the first Jewish burial in Hebron since the renewal of the community.

On the eve of Succot 5775 (2024), Staff Sergeant Yehuda Dror Yahalom of Hebron was killed in battle against Hezbollah terrorists in Lebanon. Yehuda was born a few days after the 2002 ambush on Jewish worshippers walking to Hebron for prayers on Friday evening. Among the 12 Israelis killed fighting back was Dror Weinberg, commander of the Yehuda Brigade. Yehuda Dror Yahalom was named after him and grew up in Hebron.

Two months before Yehuda was killed, he married his wife Shahar and planned to start a family and a future. The loss of Yehuda created a void and great sadness in his family and the Hebron community.

Six months later, in March of 2025, a house was purchased in Hebron by members of the Harchivi Makom Aholech organization. It is located at the top of Tel Hebron overlooking the archaeological site, adjacent to the ancient cemetery and the Biblical Tomb of Jesse and Ruth. The house was named Beit Gaon Yehuda, in memory of Yehuda Dror Yahalom and due to its geographical and historical significance at the top of Biblical Hebron, the capital of ancient Judea.

To the left of the memorial for the desecrated Torah scrolls is the modern section, established following the renewal of the Jewish community of Hebron. When more room was needed, burial continued in the northeastern section of the cemetery.

On the western side of the cemetery, to the right of the memorial for the 1929 massacre victims, there was a large section for the ancient Sephardic community of Hebron, with many hundreds of graves. These graves were desecrated and removed during the Jordanian occupation, and vegetables were planted in their place. Today, the entire section is open, as it is impossible to discern the exact location of the graves. At the edge of this section is a memorial monument erected by the descendants of the Hebron Sephardic community.

The cemetery being used as a vegetable field during the Jordanian occupation

Chabad Cemetery - Menucha Rachel Section

This section of the cemetery consisted primarily of members of the Chabad community. One of the few existing tombstones today is that of Rebbetzin Menucha Rachel Slonim. She was the granddaughter of the Alter Rebbe, the founder of the Chabad movement (Rabbi Shneur Zalman of Liadi) and daughter of the Mitteler Rebbe (Rabbi DovBer of Lubavitch). Rebbetzin Menucha Rachel was born on the 19th of Kislev 1978 (5559), the same day that her grandfather, the Alter Rebbe, was released from Russian prison. She made aliyah to Hebron with her family in the middle of the 19th century. Under her leadership, the Hebron community became the primary Chabad community in Israel at the time. The Rebbetzin was known as a miracle worker and people came to her for healing and ease of child birth. Her son, Rabbi Levi Yitzchak Slonim, is buried next to her. Many other members of the Ashkenazic community of Hebron are buried in the section.

During the Jordanian occupation, the Chabad section was completely plowed over. Most of the gravestones were removed, and a section served as a vegetable garden. Professor Ben Tzion Tavger discovered the exact site of Rebbetzin Menucha Rachel's resting place, and a monument above her grave was reconstructed.

Grave of Rebbetzin Menucha Rachel Slonim

In the Hebron Accords of 1997, this section was slated to be relinquished to the Palestinian Authority. It was only after protests and public uproar that it remained in Israeli hands. Beyond its religious and historic importance, the site is located on a strategic hilltop. When the Second Intifada broke out in September 2000 (Rosh Hashanah 5761), it became clear that the site overlooked the entire surrounding area and was vital to securing Hebron from hostile forces. Today, there is a study hall near Rebbetzin Menucha Rachel's gravesite, and many visitors come to pray at her grave throughout the year, particularly on the date of her passing, the 24th of Shevat, 1888 (5648).

Four Sites Specified in the Hebron Accords

The 1997 Hebron Accords specified four holy, historic sites, which, although designated for the PA side of the city, were supposed to be accessible to Jewish visitors. In practice, this part of the Accords has not been honored, and visits to these sites are rare if at all possible.

Map of Hebron today, including the four sites that are supposed to be accessible to Jews

Elonei Mamre

Elonei Mamre is an ancient Jewish structure from the Second Temple Era. The site is also called Abraham's Terebinth, Yerid Habotna (The pistachio tree market), and in Greek, Terebintos (oak). According to various traditions, this is the site of the Biblical Elonei Mamre where Abraham lived. There were large, impressive trees here, which, according to tradition, were identified as oak trees. A large, ancient walled area was discovered here (50 x 65 meters) that seems to have been built by King Herod and has a similar architectural style to the building above the Cave of Machpelah. Several sources identify this as the site where thousands of Jews were sold into slavery following the Bar Kochba revolt (135 BCE). In the 4th - 6th centuries, this site was home to a significant Christian landmark featuring a grandiose church. A large fair, which attracted thousands, was also held at this site.

Elonei Mamre

Cave of Otniel Ben Kenaz

According to local Jewish tradition, this is the burial place of Othniel (Otniel), son of Kenaz, the prince of the tribe of Judah, who was also the first of the Biblical Judges. The multiple tombs within the cave are identical to burial caves described in the Mishnah (Baba Batra 6:8). Over the generations, Jews have written about visits to the site, and documents show the site was purchased by Jews in the 19th century.

The cave was likely part of Hebron's ancient Jewish cemetery, which also included additional burial caves that were destroyed in the Jordanian occupation. Today, the Cave of Otniel ben Kenaz is accessible only a few times a year, on the intermediate days (*Chol Hamoed*) of Pesach and Succot, and Tisha B'Av.

Eshel Avraham

Eshel Avraham is an ancient, large, and impressive oak tree from the Middle Ages, it was called "Abraham's Oak" (*Eshel Avraham* in Hebrew). Many Jews would visit this place and enjoy the ample shade that the tree provided. The Russian Orthodox Church purchased the plot in the 19th century, and a church and monastery were built there. Access to the site was prohibited for Jews following the Hebron Accords of 1997 (5757). Later, the tree almost dried up although fresh roots grew from the ancient root, and the new sprouts continue the tradition of ancient, impressive trees that flourished in Hebron in the Biblical era.

Above: "Abraham's Oak at Hebron" (ca. 1898) by Johann Friedrich Perlberg. Below: The tree today.

Ein Sarah (Sarah's Spring)

Ein Sarah is an ancient spring and pool on the main road leading north from the Cave of Machpelah. Its structure testifies that it is an ancient mikvah, similar to those discovered in Tel Hebron, although this mikvah is larger. Above it are remnants of a public building from the Herodian era. Today, it is beneath a mosque. Many Jews of past centuries have written about their visits to the site.

Additional Sites:

Tomb of Abner (Avner) Ben Ner

According to the Bible (II Samuel, chapter 3), Abner son of Ner, head of King Saul's army, came to Hebron to make a covenant with David. However, he was killed by Joab ben Zeruiah, who suspected him of being a spy and wanted to avenge the death of his brother Asa'el. Abner was buried in Hebron while King David lamented him (II Samuel 3:33-39). This episode represented the end of the kingdom of Saul and the beginning of King David's reign over all of Israel.

Abner's Tomb was identified in the Middle Ages as being adjacent to the Tomb of the Patriarchs and Matriarchs. In the past, Jews would pray there regularly. However, after Hebron was divided in the 1990s, the Tomb of Abner was restricted to Jews, opened to them only on the ten days that the Tomb is reserved for Jewish prayers. Currently, the site is only open to Jewish prayer and study at late hours on certain weeknights.

Abner's Tomb

The Alleys of the Old City - The Casbah

Hebron's Old City and the casbah, or ancient market of Hebron, is adjacent to the Jewish quarter. It was built during the Middle Ages approximately 1,000 years ago - as opposed to the much older Tel Hebron, the site of Biblical Hebron. The Old City was built in a long process over hundreds of years, with every generation adding homes and alleyways to the existing structures. The Old City had no walls, and the houses were built closely together to create a defense system against robbers and desert marauders. This construction method created a unique and fascinating array of alleyways, courtyards, and entrances. The central alleyways were home to shops and traditional craftsmen, where one could see centuries-old production methods. The old Jewish community was also part of this tapestry. Some Jews lived in the Jewish quarter, known as the "ghetto" or "El Cortijo" neighborhood, while others lived in the alleyways outside the Jewish quarter.

Throughout the generations, the alleyways of the Old City were open to everyone – residents, craftsmen, merchants, tourists, and visitors. Even after the renewal of the Jewish community in Hebron, Jews, including children, freely walked through these alleyways. In the Hebron Accords of 1997, this area was included in H2, and Israel maintained security control over it. However, despite this, Jews were prohibited from entering (entry was allowed for members of other religions). Commerce ceased, and the majority of traditional craftsmen discontinued their activities, causing these crafts to disappear. Nowadays, these alleyways are occasionally open to Jews, under military escort, for a one-hour tour on Saturdays or for a few hours on holidays.

Simultaneously, hostile organizations and foreign governments such as Germany, France, Sweden, Norway, Turkey, Spain and others began investing immense amounts of money with the aim of erasing the Jewish history of the area and solidifying and enhancing the Arab presence. For this purpose, the HRC – Hebron Rehabilitation Committee, a branch of the Palestinian Authority, was established. This organization focuses on construction, propaganda, fundraising and more. Nonetheless, a visit to the casbah is still interesting, and remnants of the Jewish community and the ancient traditional market can still be seen. Among other things, a glass blowing workshop operates there, using ancient traditional methods.

The Triangle Gate that connected the Jewish Quarter to the alleyways of the casbah

Traditional craftsmen in Hebron at the end of the 20th century. The closure of the alleyways of the Old City destroyed a unique and historically significant cultural complex. (Photos: Yochanan Ben Yaakov)

Interesting Jewish Sites in the Casbah:

The Lintel of the Menorahs: A famous lintel adorned with the image of three menorahs, the middle one upside down, marked a Jewish building in Hebron's Casbah, and was estimated to be hundreds of years old. The menorahs symbolize the two destroyed Temples and the future reconstructed Temple. It may have been a remnant of an even older Jewish house. In the summer of 2014, the lintel was destroyed by vandals. Since then, several attempts have been made to restore it, but vandals continue to destroy the restorations.

The Lintel of the Menorahs before it was destroyed

Yehoshua Sloma Memorial Plaque: Yehoshua Sloma was a young Jewish man who immigrated to Israel from Denmark and studied at the Nir Yeshiva in Kiryat Arba. He was murdered while buying fruit in the market for the holiday of Tu B'Shvat on the 13th of Shevat, 5740 (January 31, 1980). Yehoshua was the first Jewish person murdered in Hebron since the 1929 riots. As a result of the attack, the Israeli government made the landmark decision to permanently renew the Jewish community in Hebron. The plaque memorializing him has been vandalized numerous times and repaired each time.

Yehoshua Sloma memorial plaque

Courtyard of the Kabbalists: A courtyard with Jewish residential houses marked by engraved mezuzahs on their doorways. The entrance to the courtyard bears an engraved Star of David. In the past, Jews who studied Torah and Kabbalah (mystical Jewish texts) lived and worked in this courtyard. After the 1929 massacre, the Arab residents turned the courtyard into an animal pen.

Slonim House: This is a single-story house next to the Courtyard of the Kabbalists. It was built by Levi Yitzchak Slonim, the son of Rebbetzin Menucha Rachel Slonim, the granddaughter of the Alter Rebbe of Chabad. The house was also inhabited by Rabbi Chaim Rahamim Yosef Franko (the Charif), one of the important rabbis of Hebron in the 19th and 20th centuries.

The Slonim Family, circa 1921

House of Rabbi Shimon Hausman: A prominent figure in the Hebron community in the early 20th century, Rabbi Hausman's home also served as the study house of the Karlin hasidim. The Hasson and Klonsky families lived in the northern part of the house. Today, most of the house is abandoned and part of it is damaged.

Mushayev (Mushyof) House: A unique house with a triangular facade adjacent to the Old City between Beit Romano and Beit Hadassah.

The Mushayev family were affluent and influential members of the Chabad hasidic community. The Mitteler Rebbe sent Chaim Mushayev to Hebron from Tiberias. He and his son Yosef were among the esteemed leaders of the community in the 19th century. Their home served as the meeting place for the Committee of Chabad Hasidim in Hebron and also contained a mikvah (ritual bath).

For information about sites, visiting hours, tour routes, and guided tours in Hebron, you are welcome to contact us:

office@hebron.com / Hebron Office: +972-2-996-5333
Hebron Museum: +972-72-221-3660

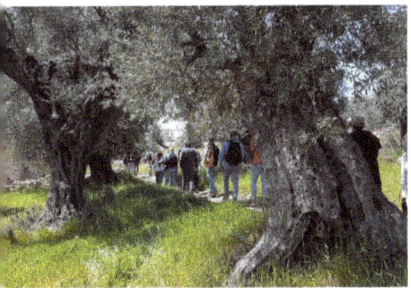

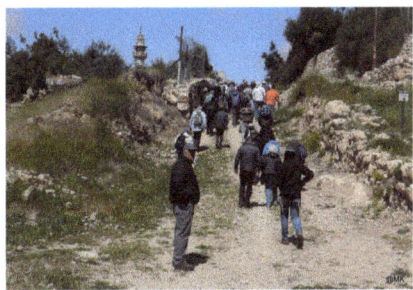

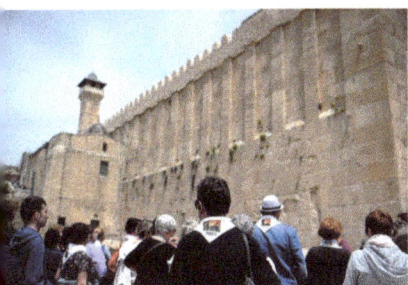

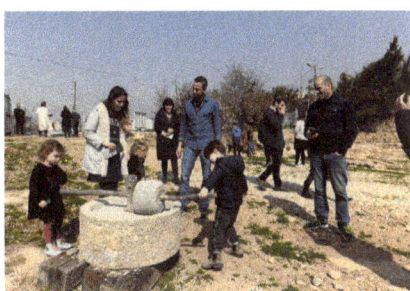

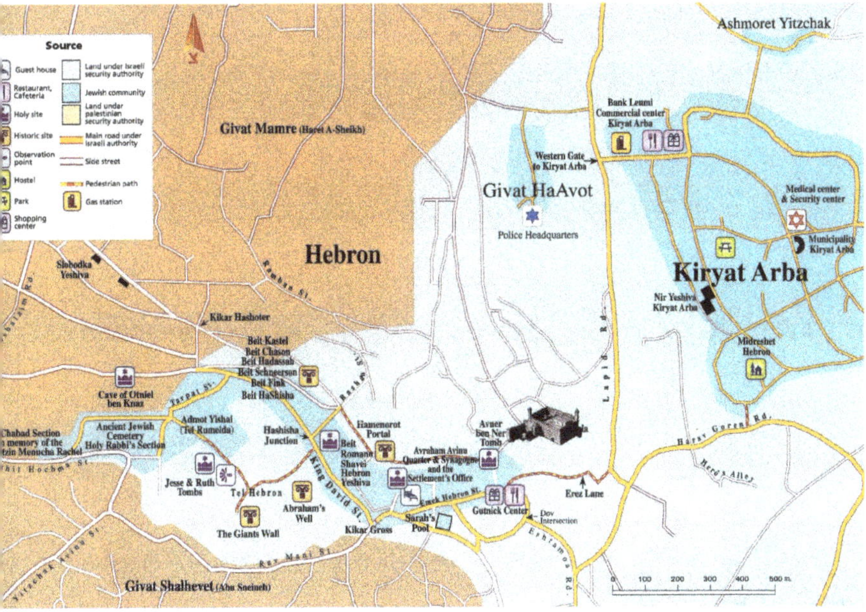
Source
Guest house
Restaurant, Cafeteria
Holy site
Historic site
Observation point
Hostel
Park
Shopping center
Land under Israeli security authority
Jewish community
Land under palestinian security authority
Main road under Israeli authority
Side street
Pedestrian path
Gas station
Givat Mamre
Hebron
Slobodka Yeshiva
Kikar Hashoter
Beit Kastel
Beit Chason
Beit Hadassah
Beit Schneerson
Beit Fink
Beit HaShisha
Cave of Otniel ben Knaz
Tarpat St.
Admot Yishai (Tel Rumeida)
Ancient Jewish Cemetery Holy Rabbi's Section
Chabad Section
Hashisha Junction
Beit Romano Shavei Hebron Yeshiva
Hamenorot Portal
Jesse & Ruth Tombs
Tel Hebron
Abraham's Well
The Giants Wall
King David St.
Kikar Gross
Sarah's Pool
Rav Mani St.
Yitzchak Avinu St.
Givat Shalhevet (Abu Sneineh)
Avraham Avinu Quarter & Synagogue and the Settlement's Office
Avner ben Ner Tomb
Emek Hebron St.
Gutnick Center
Dov Intersection
Eshtamoa Rd.
Erez Lane
Lapid Rd.
Harav Goren Rd.
Herd's Alley
0 100 200 300 400 500 m.
Ashmoret Yitzchak
Bank Leumi
Commercial center Kiryat Arba
Western Gate to Kiryat Arba
Givat HaAvot
Police Headquarters
Medical center & Security center
Municipality Kiryat Arba
Kiryat Arba
Nir Yeshiva Kiryat Arba
Midreshet Hebron

www.ingramcontent.com/pod-product-compliance
Lightning Source LLC
Chambersburg PA
CBHW050733010526
44107CB00010B/833